Make Your Dog Epic

Building an Epic Bond:
Understanding Your Dog's Training Journey

by former U.S. SBA Young Entrepreneur of the
Year, the 6x iTunes chart-topping podcast host
of the ThrivetimeShow, and *Forbes* Coaches
Council member, Clay Clark

We provide website, answer initial calls,
and branding, as well as offer other
support you can access at will.

Happy Paw·lidays

Behold, an epic, mind-expanding, dog training festival of literary wonder!

Make Your Dog Epic

ISBN: 979-8-9864278-8-1

Copyright © by Clay Clark

Clay Clark Publishing
Published by Clay Clark Publishing
3920 West 91st Street South
Tulsa, OK 74132

Endorsements
OF CLAY CLARK

"Clay, You've become an influencer. More than anything else you have evolved into an influencer where your word has more and more power. As you know there is alot of fake influencers out there. I'm glad that you and I agree so much. You are on it man! Everybody listen to this guy. He knows what he's talking about."

- Robert Kiyosaki

(The best-selling author of The Rich Dad Poor Dad book series and a man who has sold over 40 million copies of his entrepreneur books)

"Clay Clark is an entrepreneur extraordinaire."

- David Robinson

(NBA Hall of Basketball Player, former NBA MVP, NBA Championship Winner & Investor)

"He's like Steve Martin meets Steve Forbes."

- Jim Stovall

(New York Times best-selling self-help writer best known for his bestselling novel The Ultimate Gift. The book was made into the movie The Ultimate Gift, distributed by 20th Century Fox. The Ultimate Gift has a prequel called The Ultimate Life and a sequel called The Ultimate Legacy.

"For the last two years, I have come to Clay Clark's Thrivetime Show conference / seminar and I must say that I didn't know what to expect at first, but it's EXCEPTIONAL. If you are serious and I mean really serious about your career, your entrepreneurship and your wealth creation ability. I strongly, strongly implore you to come to Tulsa, invest the two days, it will change your life. It's quite extraordinary and I'm a tough grader."

- Michael Levine

(The publicist and public relations expert of choice for 58 Academy Award winners, 34 Grammy Award winners, and 43 New York Times best-sellers including Michael Jackson, Barbra Streisand, Prince, Nike and others.

PAWS, for a
Notable Quotable

"The difference between great people and
everyone else is that great people create
their lives actively, while everyone else is
created by their lives, passively waiting
to see where life takes them next. The
difference between the two is living fully
and just existing."

MICHAEL GERBER

(Best-selling author of The E-Myth Revisited)

Table of Contents

PAWS, for a
Notable Quotable

"A goal is a dream with a deadline."

NAPOLEON HILL

(The best-selling author of Think & Grow Rich)

Want to open your own Make Your Dog Epic dog training business?
Learn how to have your own epic adventure by opening one of the
most affordable and turn-key dog training businesses on the planet!

Introduction

A NOTE FROM THE FOUNDER

I want to give this short book to all of our wonderful clients, locations, and hard-working owners because I believe that it's important to be extremely transparent about how we train dogs and my proven philosophy of how we run our business.

Whether you're client seeking our expertise, a dedicated Make Your Dog Epic employee in training, a committed Make Your Dog Epic owner or simply an eager learner looking to dive into the world of dog training, know this: Our unwavering mission revolves around one singular goal—creating well-behaved, joyful dogs alongside their equally joyful owners. No one dog is the same and no one owner is the same. This is why we offer our first lesson for 50 cents. We want to figure out what it will take to get each dog to their owner's goals. The question that I thought about throughout the process of creating this system is:

> *"What's the value in a dog's obedience if it doesn't come with happiness?"*

Our goal is: "Obedience but NEVER at the expense of personality." There are many ways to train a dog and there is no regulatory body over dog training in the United States. It would be the equivalent of being a doctor, but not needing to go to school, or aspiring to be like a lawyer but the Bar Exam being voluntary.

Then even if you did take the Bar Exam, there is no governing body over it making sure they are meeting certain standards.

Basically, the point is when it comes to dog training certifications and experience don't mean anything. Because there is no governing body over certifications and they could've been doing it wrong for the last 20 years. Just because you have experience in something doesn't mean its good experience. What matters is happy customers. We pride ourselves on having the happiest clients that leave raving reviews and testimonials about us. That's all that matters. As a trainer or licensee with Make Your Dog Epic, our #1 goal is happy dogs and happy clients!

In this short training guide, I teach our training standards and the workflow that we use to actually run our business.

I am the co-founder of five kids, the former "U.S. SBA Entrepreneur of the Year" for the State of Oklahoma, the founder of several multi-million dollar companies, and the host of the ThrivetimeShow podcast which has been number one overall on the iTunes business podcast charts 6 times. I have been a member of the Forbes Business Coach Council, an Amazon best-selling author and the host of the ThrivetimeShow podcast which has hit #1 on the iTunes charts in the category of business 6 times. Throughout my career I've co-founded / founded several successful businesses including:

- » www.DJConnection.com
- » www.EpicPhotos.com
- » www.EITRLounge.com

- » www.MakeYourLifeEpic.com
- » Party Perfect (Which was purchased by Party Pro Rentals)
- » TipTopK9 Franchising (I did not start TipTopK9 Dog Training, I co-founded TipTopK9 Franchising)
- » www.Thrive15.com (The interactive online entrepreneurship school)
- » The Tulsa Bridal Association Wedding Show

Throughout my career, I have been featured in Fast Company, Bloomberg, Forbes, Entrepreneur Magazine, PandoDaily, and numerous other publications. I've been the speaker and consultant of choice for top brands throughout the country including: Hewlett Packard, Maytag University, Valspar Paint, and O'Reilly's Auto Parts. I'm also the co-founder of 5 children, the proud owner of thousands of trees, dozens of chickens, 13 cats, and one dog by the name of "Davis".

Since launching his ThrivetimeShow.com Podcast, the podcast has hit the top of the iTunes podcast charts 6 times and has featured interviews with hundreds of super successful entrepreneurs including those listed below and more:

8x New York Times Best-Selling Author and Leadership Expert, John Maxwell

Celebrity Chef, Entrepreneur, and New York Times Best-Selling Author, Wolfgang Puck

Legendary Former Key Apple Employee Turned Venture Capitalist, Best Selling Author, Guy Kawasaki

New York Times Best-Selling Co-Author of Rich Dad Poor Dad, Sharon Lechter

Senior pastor of the largest church in America with over 100,000 weekly attendees (Lifechurch.tv), Craig Groeschel

 One of America's most trusted financial experts who has written nine consecutive New York Times bestsellers with 7 million+ books in print, David Bach

 Legendary Conservative Strategist, Roger Stone

 NBA Hall of Famer, David Robinson (2-time NBA Champion, 2-time Gold Medal Winner)

 Senior Editor for Forbes and 3x Best-Selling Author, Zack O'Malley Greenburg

 Most Downloaded Business Podcaster of All-Time (EOFire. com), John Lee Dumas

 The 25th U.S. National Security Advisor and Retired U.S. Army General, Michael Flynn

 New York Times Best-Selling Author of Purple Cow, and former Yahoo! Vice President of Marketing, Seth Godin

 Co-Founder of the 700+ Employee Advertising Company (AdRoll), Adam Berke

 Emmy Award-winning Producer of the Today Show and New York Times Best-Selling Author of Sh*tty Moms, Mary Ann Zoellner

 New York Times Best-Selling Author of Contagious: Why Things Catch On and Wharton Business Professor, Jonah Berger

 New York Times Best-Selling Author of Made to Stick and Duke University Professor, Dan Heath

 International Best-Selling Author of In Search of Excellence, Tom Peters

 NBA Player and Coach, Muggsy Bogues (Shortest player to ever play in the league)

 NFL Running Back, Rashad Jennings (and Winner of Dancing with the Stars)

Lee Cockerell (The former Executive Vice President of Walt Disney World who once managed 40,000 employees)

 Michael Levine (PR consultant of choice for Michael Jackson, Prince, Nike, Charlton Heston, Nancy Kerrigan, etc.)

 Billboard Contemporary Christian Top 40 Recording Artist, Colton Dixon

 Conservative Talk Pundit, Frequent Fox News Contributor, Political Commentator and Best-Selling Author, Ben Shapiro

See additional guests at
ThrivetimeShow.com

Make Your Life Epic is a business consulting practice where I and my team coach 160 business owners every month in many different industries. The systems we recommend at Make Your Dog Epic are the same systems used in all industries to make them successful.

 *"When you WOW your clients they will refer you close to now." -Clay Clark*

Do you own a business? Well, I have a long track record of helping people to grow businesses using best-practice systems, processes, checklists, strategies and moves that I use. Thousands of our client success stories can be found at: www.ThrivetimeShow.com. So what is Make Your Life Epic? Make Your Life Epic is a best-practice business growth consulting company where I and my team coach 160 business owners in many different industries. The systems we use at Make Your Dog Epic are the same proven systems that I teach our clients to make them successful.

READ CLAY CLARK'S BOOK(S):

Download Clay Clark's Books for Free at:
https://www.ThrivetimeShow.com/free-resources

CLAY IS THE AUTHOR OF 20+ BOOKS INCLUDING:

A MILLIONAIRE'S GUIDE TO BECOMING SUSTAINABLY RICH
The World's Best Business Growth & Consulting Book: Business Growth Strategies from the World's Best Business Coach.

F6 JOURNAL
Meta Thrive Time Journal.

BOOM
The 14 Proven Steps to Business Success.

WHEEL OF WEALTH
An Entrepreneur's Action Guide.

JACKASSARY
Jackassery will serve as a beacon of light for other entrepreneurs that are looking to avoid troublesome employees and difficult situations. This is real. This is raw. This is unfiltered entrepreneurship.

THE ENTREPRENEUR'S DRAGON ENERGY
The Mindset Kanye, Trump and You Need to Succeed.

MAKE YOUR LIFE EPIC
Clay shares his journey and struggle from the dorm room to the board room during his raw and action-packed story of how he built DJConnection.com.

THRIVE
How to Take Control of Your Destiny and Move Beyond Surviving... Now!

THE ART OF GETTING THINGS DONE
Time-tested Super moves that you can use to create both the time freedom and financial freedom that most people only dream about.

SALES DOMINATION
Clay Clark is a master of selling and now he wants to teach you his proven processes, scalable systems and sales mastery moves in a humorous and practical way.

ENTREPRENEURSHIP: SIMPLIFIED, AMPLIFIED, & VISUALIZED
Throughout my career, I have been blessed to achieve tremendous success both as an entrepreneur and as a podcast host.

WILL NOT WORK FOR FOOD
9 Big Ideas for Effectively Managing Your Business in an Increasingly Dumb, Distracted & Dishonest America.

HOW TO REPEL FRIENDS AND NOT INFLUENCE PEOPLE
The epic whale of a tale featuring America's self proclaimed most humble male.

DON'T LET YOUR EMPLOYEES HOLD YOU HOSTAGE
This candid book shares how to avoid being held hostage by employees.

IT'S NOT LONELY AT THE TOP
15 Keys to achieving a successful, peaceful, and drama-free life. (3/4 of this book is handwritten by Clay Clark, himself).

TRADE-UPS
Learn how to design and live the life you love, how to find and create the time needed to get things done in a world filled with endless digital distractions, and more!

IF MY WALLS COULD TALK
The Notes, Quotes, & Epiphanies I've Written On Clay's Office Walls. (Hardcover).

SEARCH ENGINE DOMINATION
Learn the Proven System We've Used to Earn Millions.

PODCAST DOMINATION 101
This book will show you how to prepare, record, launch, and begin generating income from your podcast, all from your home studio!

Want to open your own Make Your Dog Epic dog training business?
Learn how to have your own epic adventure by opening one of the most affordable and turn-key dog training businesses on the planet!

A NOTE FROM OUR BOISE
LOCATION, OWNER & TRAINER.

Thank You for striving to Make Your Dog Epic! No matter what, life is about goals, lessons and learning. And isn't that such a great and wonderful thing!? It allows us to take things less seriously and have some fun whiling away at the lessons we don't know we have the opportunity to learn.
Each dog provides us with new opportunities to learn and grow with them.

After training over 2,000 dogs over 6+ years, we are still learning lessons to this day! Dogs are the most marvelous and inspiring, heartwarming companions we could ever dream of.

Your experience with training should be lessons for you and your dog, and there are always more lessons to learn. Learning, as most of us know, can take effort, patience, mistakes, time, energy, effort, and a lot of help! It can seem daunting or confusing at times because it's so new! That is part of the process and you will be glad you stayed the course!

It also gives us understanding, patience, love, compassion, understanding, empathy, skills, tools, wisdom, knowledge, experience, results, and so much more!!

As the committed student you are, please remember, we are here for you and to help you! Whether it is something you want to hear or not, we are here to find solutions that work for you, your dog, and your lives together. Through practice makes progress and we always want to be enabling you to progress together.

Your bond with your dog and the amount of freedom through discipline and understanding will grow together and we want to be part of that journey with you.

Every human is different, every dog is different, and every lifestyle is different. Our training can fit into whatever that combination looks like for your family.

You inspire us to continue to be better. You bring joy to our day by enabling us to spend time with you and your pups every day!

Our team is your support system and will always have your best interest at heart as long as you need us. We thrive and are delighted in seeing you and your dog have more understanding and joy together!

In your corner through this world of companion learning and joy,

Sincerely,
Darcy Denton-Heise

PAWS, for a
Notable Quotable

"We all get good ideas at seminars and
from books and business-building gurus.
The problem is that most companies
do not know how to identify and adapt
the best ideas to their businesses.
Implementation, not ideas, is the key
to real success."

CHET HOMES

*(The best-selling author of The Ultimate Sales Machine
and legendary business growth consultant)*

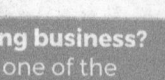

CHAPTER 1

The Power of the Weekly Meeting

(DEPENDABILITY IS THE MOST IMPORTANT ABILITY)

At Make Your Dog Epic, we schedule a weekly, one-hour, recurring meeting where we look at big wins of the week, the status of our team's key performance indicators, any big issues or burning fires that need to be resolved, following up on the status of action items from last week, assigning action items for the following week, and situational dog training.

The items we typically cover in our weekly meeting include:

- » Big wins of the week
- » The vision of Make Your Life Epic Dog Training
- » The status of our key performance indicators (quantifiable numbers and key performance metrics)
- » Burning fires
- » Follow-up action items (did everyone get their assignments done?)
- » Assign action items (who, what, when, where, why?)

Our commitment to follow this agenda each week will keep our company from ever drifting too far away from our core customers, our core vision, our core brand and our core values.

PAWS, for a
Notable Quotable

"Drifting, without aim or purpose, is the first cause of failure."

NAPOLEON HILL
(Best-selling author of Think & Grow Rich)

CHAPTER 2

Tracking

(WHY WE MUST MEASURE WHAT WE TREASURE)

We track multiple metrics every single week. It's vital for the business and customer satisfaction that we track our daily and weekly key performance indicators.

A few of the weekly metrics we track are:

1. Leads
2. Where leads are coming from - (advertising sources, word of mouth, etc)
3. Leads booked
4. Leads sold
5. How much cash we received
6. How much we did in sales
7. How much we are spending on advertising
8. Cost per click with advertising
9. How many objective Google reviews we received
10. How many video testimonials we received
11. How long its taking employees to train dogs
12. How much each dog is progressing per day
13. Tracking how long it takes for our Boarding School Packages to be properly trained
14. Tracking how long it take for each trainer to train dogs
15. Etc.

By holding our team accountable for tracking our daily key performance indicators, we can keep our finger on the pulse of the business without having to be there with each member of our team, holding them accountable during every moment of their work day. As an owner, there are many things that go on during your day to day. You can not hold the hand of every employee at all times. So you must have the systems and processes in place while tracking all key performance indicators to hold them accountable.

PAWS, for a
Notable Quotable

"Measure what you treasure. What you track won't be allowed to slack."

CLAY CLARK

(Former Oklahoma Young U.S. SBA Entrepreneur of the Year)

CHAPTER 3

Don't Reinvent the Wheel

**(FOLLOW THE PROVEN PROCESSES
& SUCCESS SYSTEMS)**

As an owner of a Make Your Dog Epic licensed business, I would highly recommend that you follow the proven-turn-key and best-practice systems that I have developed. However, because you are a licensee and not a franchisee, I cannot demand that you do. However, as a client of one of our locations, and seeing as you pay us and not the other way around, my hope is that we can WOW you so that you can see the value of implementing our proven systems and processes.

I know that as a dog owning consumer you are constantly bombarded with social media videos, self-proclaimed dog training experts, and your mother-in-law, all telling you how you should train your dog. However, when you invest in us, we are committed to wowing you so that you are happy to tell your family and friends about the quality of the results that we delivered.

To the dog trainers: I would highly recommend that you follow best-practice systems as opposed to guessing, hoping and wishing that through the process of entropy, success will magically appear. Your goal is to create happy customers and happy dogs.

To Make Your Dog Epic location owners: we have made this business and the dog training ownership as empowering, simple, and easy as possible by supporting you as a trainer.

PAWS, for a
Notable Quotable

"The size of your success is measured by the strength of your desire; the size of your dream; and how you handle disappointment along the way."

ROBERT KIYOSAKI

(The best-selling author of the Rich Dad Poor Dad book series, the host of the Rich Dad Radio Show and a man who has sold over 45 million copies of his self-help books, and a guest on Clay Clark's ThrivetimeShow)

CHAPTER 4
The Carrot & F.O.C.U.S.

(FOCUS ON CORE TASKS UNTIL SUCCESS PHILOSOPHY)

When you are growing a business, most of the time it isn't necessary to reinvent the wheel. Most things have already been done so you must simply study the proven processes and best-practice systems. That is what we have done at Make Your Dog Epic. Since 1999 I have seen and built many different businesses in many different industries. I have seen many different methods, systems, and philosophies in dog training. Whether it is classical conditioning, operant conditioning, positive reinforcement, negative reinforcement, escape learning, avoidance learning, balanced training, attention based training, addition of stimulus, or removal of a stimulus, I have studied many different dog training methods.

When training dogs we don't want dogs to be reliant on treats. As an example, when you have an employee who works for $___ per hour, which is great and it motivates them to do it. However they are expecting a paycheck. If they don't receive the paycheck they are going to think "Why am I doing this?" Then, eventually, they will just stop going to work. Additionally, if the employee sees another job is hiring for 2 times what you are paying per hour and it's going to be more fun they will usually take that job immediately. This is because people without loyalty will immediately pick the higher value object without even trying to create a win-win and sustainable relationship with their boss.

At Make Your Dog Epic, we know of many of the different popular styles and methodologies that exist within the dog training world. We also believe every single training method has its pros and its cons, for the dog and for the owner as well. At Make Your Dog Epic we have created a dog training company where our goal is to take the best trainers, support them to do what they do best—train! When you combine that with including a positive experience with each dog, you can't go wrong. The result is that we have created a company of dog trainers that we truly believe to be all-around the best for the dogs and great humans like you.

We endorse a hybrid of training we refer to as "Focused-Based Positive Reinforcement Training." We also refer to it as "The Carrot & F.O.C.U.S. (Focus On Core Tasks Until Success) Philosophy." The simplified explanation of this training is that the goal is focus and movement from the dog. So we want to gain the dog's focus and teach it the movement we are doing and then repeat, repeat, repeat, until the dog understands it. Then we reward the dog with positive reinforcement once they have done something satisfactorily.

At Make Your Dog Epic, we know of many of the different popular styles and methodologies that exist within the dog training world, however we are both dreamers and doers at Make Your Dog Epic. We aspire to WOW our customers and to create an enjoyable training experience for both the dogs and the dog trainers. We also believe every single training method has its pros and cons, for the dog and for the owner as well. However, our focus is to provide you and your dog with a positive experience, and thus the best-way to do that is for us to demonstrate for you in person our dog training system and that is why the first lesson with Make Your Dog Epic is always just 50 cents.

PAWS, for a
Notable Quotable

"Drifting, without aim or purpose, is the first cause of failure."

NAPOLEON HILL

(The best-selling author of Think & Grow Rich)

PAWS, for a
Notable Quotable

"All successful people men and women are big dreamers. They imagine what their future could be, ideal in every respect, and then they work every day toward their distant vision, that goal or purpose."

BRIAN TRACY

(Best-selling author, world-class trainer, motivational speaker and sales trainer)

CHAPTER 5

The B.O.O.M. Method Explained

In order to establish ourselves as the best dog trainers in the world we have created a simple, but effective dog training methodology known as B.O.O.M. This is a great mindset to train with.

BOOM

1. Big expectations
2. Overwhelming encouragement
3. Optimistic and consistent feedback
4. More repetition until mastery occurs

When you bring your dog for the very first 50 cent lesson and dog training session with one of our locations, you will immediately witness the professionalism, skills and mastery of the dog trainers we choose to team up with. As you watch us utilize proven best-practice dog training methods your mind will be so blown away that you may want to wrap your head in duct tape.

Big expectations - We set massive expectations for both ourselves and the dogs we train. Imagine having a world-class trainer train your dog so that they can have UNLIMITED OFF-leash freedom! Our goal is for your dog to listen to the first command every time. When they do this your dog will have more freedom which equals a better life.

Overwhelming encouragement - If your dog does a command to satisfaction we shower them with positive reinforcements with either treats or praise or both! That way the training environment is not only mentally stimulating for your dog, but also super fun.

Optimistic and consistent feedback - No matter where your dog is training, your dog is going to need optimistic and consistent feedback. If the dog does not do the command we are never mad. However we have to be consistent with the focused attention and showing the dog the correct behavior. We must set up the best learning environment for your dog.

More repetition until mastery occurs - Just like learning how to play the piano, growing a garden or growing a business, teaching your dog how to become well behaved requires discipline, focus and more repetition until mastery occurs. However, when you hire Make Your Dog Epic dog training you do not have to invest your personal time to train your dog how to become well behaved, because that is what we do.

PAWS, for a
Notable Quotable

"Practice does not make perfect. Only perfect practice makes perfect."

VINCE LOMBARDI

(A man recognized as one of the greatest coaches in American football history)

Want to open your own Make Your Dog Epic dog training business?
Learn how to have your own epic adventure by opening one of the most affordable and turn-key dog training businesses on the planet!

PAWS, for a Notable Quotable

"BE LIKE A POSTAGE STAMP. STICK TO IT UNTIL YOU GET THERE."
—HARVEY MACKAY

DETER MEND
MEDIOCRITY PL.
NOWHERE, UTAH

CLAY CLARK
777 SUCCESS AVE.
74119 TULSA, OK

(An American business man, author, and columnist. The best-selling author of seven New York times best-selling books.)

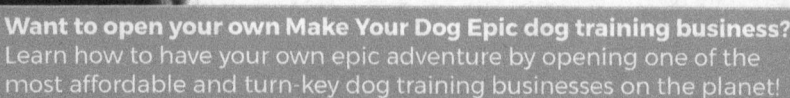

CHAPTER 6
The Group Interview

(WHY NOTHING WILL WORK, IF WE WON'T)

As an owner, hiring can be one of the most frustrating things. I'm busy and you're busy, but you and I must block off time to conduct weekly interviews to find people who will best represent your company. I love scheduling group interviews because it saves time and allows me to see how candidates compare with each other in a literal side-by-side comparison (A tryout of sorts). If you don't want to do group interviews, then you are going to have to block out many hours throughout your week to interview potential candidates who might or might not show up on time or at all for their interviews. Because I realize that 40% of potential candidates don't have the mental capacity or the diligence needed to actually show up on time for their initial interviews, I love the group interview format. When someone responds to a job post, our team schedules them for an interview.

PAWS, for a
Notable Quotable

"The time that leads to mastery is dependent on the intensity of our focus."

ROBERT GREENE

(Best-selling author of Mastery, The 50th Law, The Law of Human Nature & The 48 Laws of Power)

"75% of employees steal from the workplace and most do so repeatedly." - U.S. Department of Commerce.

https://www.forbes.com/sites/ivywalker/2018/12/28/your-employees-are-probably-stealing-from-you-here-are-five-ways-to-put-an-end-to-it/?sh=42cda3863386

"32% of employees are engaged in the workplace." - Gallup

https://www.shrm.org/resourcesandtools/hr-topics/behavioral-competencies/global-and-cultural-effectiveness/pages/new-gallup-poll-employee-disengagement-hits-9-year-high.aspx

During an interview, many business owners spend massive quantities of time going on and on about their company and their vision while the candidates sit quietly, scanning the room for a blunt object with which they can respectfully bash in their skull to stop the boredom. Candidates begin to feel as though the person interviewing them has no gameplan or agenda, because they don't. To make matters worse, most companies delegate the recruitment and interviewing process to "the new guy" or the person on your staff who hasn't quite found his place within your company culture. This is terrible. My friend, the person conducting the interviews must look sharp and must be a confidence-inspiring powerhouse who can follow the perfect interview agenda every time which includes:

- Clarifying the goals of the company
- Clarifying the goals of the candidate
- Clarifying the expectations of the job
- Clarify the compensation of the job
- Clarifying the career path of the job
- Answering any questions
- Clarifying the next steps for the applicants

When hiring you are looking for the 4 E's

» Energy – Does the candidate have the energy to bring enthusiasm to the workplace every day?

» Energize – Does the candidate have the ability to energize those around him or her?

» Edge – Does the candidate have the edge needed to make the tough decisions?

» Execute – Does the candidate have the ability to execute and actually get their job done?

» BONUS – I have also found that it is extremely important that you search for candidates who are coachable.

PAWS, for a
Notable Quotable

"If you pick the right people and give them the opportunity to spread their wings and put compensation as a career behind it you almost don't have to manage them."

JACK WELCH

*(The former CEO who grew GE by 4,000%
during his tenure at GE)*

"ENTREPRENEURS SOLVE THE WORLD'S PROBLEMS
AND UNAPOLOGETICALLY MAKE MONEY DOING IT."
– CLAY CLARK

"Don't be an ASK Hole."

Ask·hole [ask-hole]

noun

1. A person who asks questions, yet doesn't want to know the answers.

2. A person who chooses to not have the mental capacity and tenacity needed to implement proven systems.

3. A person who refuses to bore down and do the work because they struggle with perpetual boredom.

CHAPTER 7

☆ ☆ ☆ ☆ ☆

Gather Objective Google Reviews from Happy Customers

(WHY YOUR ONLINE REPUTATION DETERMINES THE AMOUNT OF YOUR COMPENSATION)

As I said earlier there is no governing body over dog training so what people say about you and how good of a job you do really does matter. Gathering objective reviews from your current & past customers is one of the most important things you could do in any business not to mention a industry that the only thing showing you do a good job is your past customers. In fact, around the year 2017 I had the opportunity to work with a couple whose business was stuck every year at approximately $400,000 per year of annual revenue. However, within just one short year we helped them to grow from $400,000 to $598,000 in annual revenue. In fact, this couple that I was working with was actually resorting to buying fake awards when I first met them in order to convince their customers of their legitimacy which is ironic; When meeting a potential client bring our own dogs to show people what you can do. Your past customers are the only thing that can truly show people what you can do.

You cannot afford to sit back and wait for objective Google reviews to flow in and to come to you. Go get those reviews from your real customers. Once you have the most objective Google reviews from your current and former clients you will climb to the top of Google search results quickly. Most business owners fail here by passively waiting for their customers to provide them with reviews and acting as though the negative reviews that have been written don't impact the buying decisions of potential customers. In this world of anonymous reviews, the trolls can quickly gain control, so you must proactively e-mail, call, and ask your happy customers to write a review for you. Competitors, former employees, and people that you decided not to hire will actually invest the time needed to give you bad reviews.

Most sane people will not typically go out of their way to request reviews. If you are not proactive about asking for reviews from your happy customers, you will wake up one morning and discover that you have four negative reviews and no positive reviews.

Years ago, I worked with a couple of clients who would always talked about how God was going to bless them because they were believers in Jesus and the prosperity mindset.

PAWS, for a
Notable Quotable

"Mediocre people suffer from boredom
while the greats bore down."

CLAY CLARK

However, these two clients refused to get more than 3-5 objective reviews per week from their real customers.

After investing a copious amount of time with those two clients I was able to finally convince them, although God wanted to bless them, in order for them to get to the top of the Google search engine algorithm they would need to gather the most Google reviews in their service area. As a result of embracing implementing this concept and many other proven, best-practice systems, this super-appreciative client was able to grow their stagnant business from 1 location to 15+ locations.

PAWS, for a
Notable Quotable

"In a crowded marketplace, fitting in is failing. In a busy marketplace, not standing out is the same as being invisible."

SETH GODIN

(Seth Godin is an author, entrepreneur and most of all, a teacher. Seth is an entrepreneur, best-selling author, and speaker)

CHAPTER 8

Gather Objective Video Reviews from Happy Customers

(WHY REAL HUMANS ON THE REAL PLANET EARTH MUST ACTUALLY ENDORSE THE SERVICE WE PROVIDE)

People need to see video testimonials from your real customers that you are actually working with. I cannot say it enough how valuable getting video reviews from your real customers is!. If you're reading this as a client and you own a business immediately go out and get 100 Google reviews and 100 video reviews from your happy customers and post them everywhere. People need to see that your customers are SUPER happy about the services you have provided.

A note for our trainers and owners if you do not feel like our customer would say good things on a Google review or a video review you yourself did something wrong. Customers should be ecstatic after training with you. You should've just changed their life! The difference between a well-trained dog and an untrained dog can be someone's sanity!

PAWS, for a
Notable Quotable

"The Tiffany Theory states that a gift delivered in a box from Tiffany's will have a higher perceived value than one in no box or a plain box. That's not because the recipient is a fool; it's because in our society, we gift-wrap everything: our politicians, our corporate heads, our movie and TV stars, and even our toilet paper. Public Relations is like gift wrapping."

MICHAEL LEVINE

(Best-selling author and the PR consultant of choice for Michael Jackson, Pizza Hut, Nike, Prince, and a multiple-time guest on the ThrivetimeShow podcast.)

BUSINESS 101

CHAPTER 9

Never-Stop Advertising

(WITHOUT LEADS YOUR BUSINESS WILL BLEED)

If you are the top dog trainer in the world and do a better job than anyone in the history of dog training that's great, but it does not matter at all if you do not have leads. That is exactly why we choose to throw our brand name behind passionate trainers like you! We want to magnify great dog trainers. It does not matter if you are a good salesperson if you don't have leads. It does not matter If you have motivational quotes all over your facility if you do not have leads. It is very simple: your business bleeds if you do not have leads. In a perfect world, you wouldn't have to spend money on marketing to new customers and word of mouth would organically make your business grow exponentially forever.

The reality, however, whether you are Nike, McDonald's, Southwest Airlines, or Disney World, you are going to have to invest in consistent advertising to stay in the minds of your ideal and likely buyers. The big question is this: how much money does it cost your company to attract one customer? This is where a tracking program comes in. You want to track your leads. Where are your leads coming from? How many leads are you getting per week?

PAWS, for a Notable Quotable

"Unless you value yourself, you will not value your time, and you will not do anything with it."

CLAY CLARK

(6X iTunes chart-topping podcast host and the co-creator of five human kids)

PAWS, for a
Notable Quotable

"It takes a lot of hard work to make something simple, to truly understand the underlying challenges and come up with elegant solutions. Simplicity is the ultimate sophistication...That's been one of my mantras – focus and simplicity. Simple can be harder than complex: You have to work hard to get your thinking clean to make it simple. But it's worth it in the end because once you get there, you can move mountains."

STEVE JOBS
(The co-founder of Apple, the founder of NeXT, and the former CEO of PIXAR)

CHAPTER 10

Our Commitment to Training

Our commitment is that is that we will be there for training even after you've completed your classes. We train many dogs that have trained with other trainers, however, those who train with us never train anywhere else. Not necessarily because we are superior trainers, but because we will be there for the rest of your dog's life! With numerous dog trainers, training tools, methods, myths, and misconceptions out there, we are honored that you chose us to embark on this journey with you and your pup.

We will help you and your dog to achieve your specific goals. We understand that all dogs are unique, and everyone has distinct objectives with their pup. Whatever those goals may be, we will guide you to reach them. We offer a money-back guarantee, and we will NEVER shift blame to you if the training doesn't work; it will always be our responsibility!

No matter which training program you choose with us, group classes are included for FREE for the rest of your dog's life. That's because we want to be there for the entirety of your dog's life! Let's make your dog EPIC!"

Clay Clark
- Founder of MakeYourDogEpic.com

"I've been screwed, I've had millions of dollars embezzled from me and I've had ungrateful partners push me out of their businesses after I've helped them to grow their business by 18x without apology simply to increase their income and at the end of the day we must all choose to become bitter or better or over time we will become so cold that we should wear a sweater."

CLAY CLARK

(6X iTunes chart-topping podcast host and the co-creator of five human kids)

PAWS, for a Notable Quotable

"Before success comes in any man's life, he is sure to meet with much temporary defeat, and, perhaps, some failure. When defeat overtakes a man, the easiest and most logical thing to do is to quit. That is exactly what the majority of men do. More than five hundred of the most successful men this country has ever known told the author their greatest success came just one step beyond the point at which defeat had overtaken them."

NAPOLEON HILL

(The best-selling author of Think & Grow Rich)

CHAPTER 11:
Dog Math

How long does it take to train your dog?

Most wonderful people like you that allow us to train their dog want to know how long the proper training of your dog is going to take? And that is a valid question that I will attempt to answer with the following DOG MATH equations:

Dog Training Time Required
Example Packages:

- 🐾 The Basic Package = 1 Week of Training
- 🐾 The Advanced Package = 2 Weeks of Training
- 🐾 The Epic Package = 3 Weeks of Training

Whether we are talking about training dogs or teaching humans to speak Spanish, everyone learns at a different pace. However, once we are confident that your dog has been well-

PAWS, for a
Notable Quotable

"Running a successful business requires Three P's: Planning, Procedures & Policies."

CHET HOLMES

(The best-selling author of The Ultimate Sales Machine and a legendary business growth consultant before the time of his death.)

trained we offer on-going and perpetual training for the rest of your dog's life so that you as an owner and they as the dog can get additional training and tune ups on dog skills on a weekly basis.

PAWS, for a Notable Quotable

"I realized that becoming a master of karate was not about learning 4,000 moves but about doing just a handful of moves 4,000 times."

CHET HOLMES

(The best-selling author of The Ultimate Sales Machine and a legendary business growth consultant before the time of his death.)

How long does it take to train your employees and local owners to become dog trainers?

If you are familiar with dogs and are a very physically coordinated individual we believe that it will take you approximately 8 weeks of on-site training to learn how to become a dog trainer depending where you receive your training from. However, if you already skilled at training dogs it may be much faster. The following skills will be helpful to you as a location owner:

 How a Workflow Works
 How to Properly Train Dogs
 How to Train Dog Trainers

- 🐾 How to Conduct Weekly Group Job Interviews
- 🐾 How to Conduct Your Weekly Staff Meeting
- 🐾 How to Conduct Your Daily Staff Huddles
- 🐾 How to Manage Your Time And Block Out Your Calendar Effectively
- 🐾 How to Manage Your Team (Master the Art of Follow-up)
- 🐾 How to On-Board New Employees
- 🐾 How to Fire Employees That Refuse to Follow Your Dog Training Systems
- 🐾 How to Optimize Your Local Internet Presence
- 🐾 How to Optimize Your Local Google Map
- 🐾 How Online Reputation Works
- 🐾 How Online Advertising Works
- 🐾 How to Track Your Weekly Numbers
- 🐾 How to Sell In the Win-Win Manner That We Recommend (we do not believe in using high-pressure sales techniques, and not using various manipulative sales strategies)

If you are interested in becoming a Make Your Dog Epic business owner, we would love to speak with you. We are currently the most affordable dog training business opportunity on the planet. To schedule a free consultation simply find the "Want to Open a Make Your Dog Epic Business/Location?" button which is found under the "Locations" button on the website. You can also simply fill out the "CONTACT" button which is found on our website at: https://MakeYourDogEpic.com/Contact/

"Having grown thousands of businesses, I believe that anyone teaching highly manipulative sales techniques, whether they have a beard or not, is a modern pirate and a sick, twisted freak. It does not matter to me whether someone is suffering from "little-king" syndrome or they are just a timid, cowardly, and weak force individually. Any sales person who actually devotes time every week to learn and train himself and his team how to implement highly manipulative sales techniques is not one with purity and not someone with whom I would do business. He is someone that is likely to introduce his second wife on the next episode of "Jerry Springer." - Clay Clark

Want to open your own Make Your Dog Epic dog training business?
Learn how to have your own epic adventure by opening one of the most affordable and turn-key dog training businesses on the planet!

TRAINING SUCCESS TIP!

CHAPTER 12:

The 10 Rules of Puppy Potty Training Success

Unless you hate your life and want your home to smell like dog excrement, potty training your puppy is a crucial step in raising a well-behaved and happy puppy. Establishing a consistent routine, using positive reinforcement, and understanding your puppy's cues are the keys to success in this endeavor.

In this guide (easy to use ULTIMATE POTTY TRAINING GUIDE) we will walk you through a very simple process to make potty training easier and more effective, along with some do's and don'ts to ensure a smooth journey. Remember, patience and consistency is your best friend during this process of potty training man's best friend. The process is very simple. However, it's tedious and slightly annoying, but less annoying than cleaning up the constant dog urine and poop that will be flowing through your house if you do not become proactive about potty training your puppy.

RULE #1 - Begin Your Day Early

NOTE: START YOUR DAY BY TAKING YOUR PUPPY OUTSIDE IN THE MORNING.

NOTE: PUPPIES CAN USUALLY HOLD THEIR
BLADDER FOR ABOUT SEVEN HOURS AT NIGHT,
SO THIS MORNING TRIP SETS THE TONE FOR
THE DAY AND HELPS ESTABLISH A ROUTINE.

RULE #2 - Use Same Spot Each Time

NOTE: TAKE THE PUPPY TO THE SAME SPOT
EACH TIME

You want to take your puppy to the same spot every single time they go out to potty. With dogs the key is repetition until it becomes a habit.

NOTE: NO EXPLORATION UNTIL
AFTER THEY POTTY

RULE #3 - Use a Leash

NOTE: TAKE YOUR DOG OUT ON A LEASH
SO YOU CAN ENSURE THEY ARE NOT JUST
RUNNING AROUND CHEWING UP STICKS. AFTER
THEY POTTY YOU'RE WELCOME TO LET THEM
OFF LEASH AND THEY CAN RUN AROUND.

RULE #4 -
Positive Reinforcement Matters

NOTE: PRAISE YOUR PUPPY WHEN THEY POTTY CORRECTLY

NOTE: PRAISE YOUR PUPPY ENTHUSIASTICALLY EVERY TIME THEY USE THE DESIGNATED POTTY SPOT. YOU CAN ALSO OFFER A TREAT TO REINFORCE THE BEHAVIOR AND MAKE IT MORE ENJOYABLE. THE KEY IS GIVE THE TREAT RIGHT AFTER THEY GO POTTY. DO NOT WAIT UNTIL YOU GO BACK INSIDE. IF YOU WAIT THEY WILL THINK THEY GET A TREAT FOR JUST GOING OUTSIDE.

RULE #5 -
Master the Power of the Crate

NOTE: YOU SHOULD ONLY GIVE YOUR DOGS 10-15 MIN MAXIMUM TO POTTY OUTSIDE. IF THEY DO NOT POTTY YOU NEED TO TAKE THEM BACK INSIDE AND PUT THEM IN THE CRATE FOR 30 MIN AND THEN TRY AGAIN. THIS IS WHERE IT GETS TEDIOUS BECAUSE YOU NEED TO DO THIS OVER AND OVER.

NOTE: Size of the crate matters

NOTE: The crate needs to be small enough that your puppy can not pee or poop on one side of the kennel and lay on the other.

RULE #6 -
You Must Observe the 30-Minute Rule

NOTE: Expect your puppy to need another potty break about 30 minutes after eating or drinking.

NOTE: This timing becomes an essential part of the routine.

RULE #7 -
Consistency Is Key

NOTE: Always take your puppy to the same designated potty spot.

NOTE: BY CONSISTENTLY USING THIS AREA, YOUR PUPPY WILL LEARN THAT THIS IS THE RIGHT PLACE TO GO.

RULE #8 - Using Commands

NOTE: SELECT A SPECIFIC COMMAND TO ASSOCIATE WITH POTTY TIME, SUCH AS "GO POTTY" OR "DO YOUR BUSINESS." THIS COMMAND WILL HELP YOUR PUPPY UNDERSTAND THE DESIRED BEHAVIOR.

RULE #9 - Repetition

NOTE: REPEAT THE CHOSEN COMMAND. IT MAY TAKE SOME TIME FOR YOUR PUPPY TO CONNECT THE COMMAND WITH THE ACTION, SO BE PATIENT.

RULE #10 - Bad News, Some dogs don't have full bladder control until they are 8 months old and some humans lose all bladder control after spending a night out partying. Don't let your dog binge-drink & party all night.

Frequently Asked Questions

HOW LONG DOES POTTY TRAINING TAKE?

Potty training duration varies depending on age, breed, and temperament of the dog. It can take a few weeks to up to six months for complete potty training.

HOW DO I RECOGNIZE WHEN MY PUPPY NEEDS TO GO?

Watch for signs like whining, barking, restlessness, pacing, sniffing, or circling. These cues indicate that your puppy needs a potty break. WARNING. Your dog might start training you to get attention from mom or dad. So make sure you go out with a leash and to the same spot. If your dog doesn't potty it goes back in the crate for 30 minutes.

HOW SHOULD I HANDLE MISTAKES?

React calmly and never punish your puppy for accidents. Interrupt them if you catch them in the act and take them to the designated potty spot. Clean accidents thoroughly to remove odors. Never leave copious amounts of urine and dog feces around your home, never live with twelve dogs and don't become a hoarder. Also, choose now to never become weak, feeble, weakened, frail, soft, wimpish, slight, tender, lame, wimpy, passiveaggressive, and a double-minded, back-stabbing, greedy person.

AREN'T CRATES BAD?

Absolutely not. Crates are a great tool to use for potty training. To help your dog like the crate you can feed them inside the crate with the door shut. You may also put them in the crate randomly throughout the day for 30 seconds, 3 minutes, 10 min, etc not just when you are going to leave the house for hours. That way your pup doesn't think they are going to be in the crate for hours anytime they are put in it.

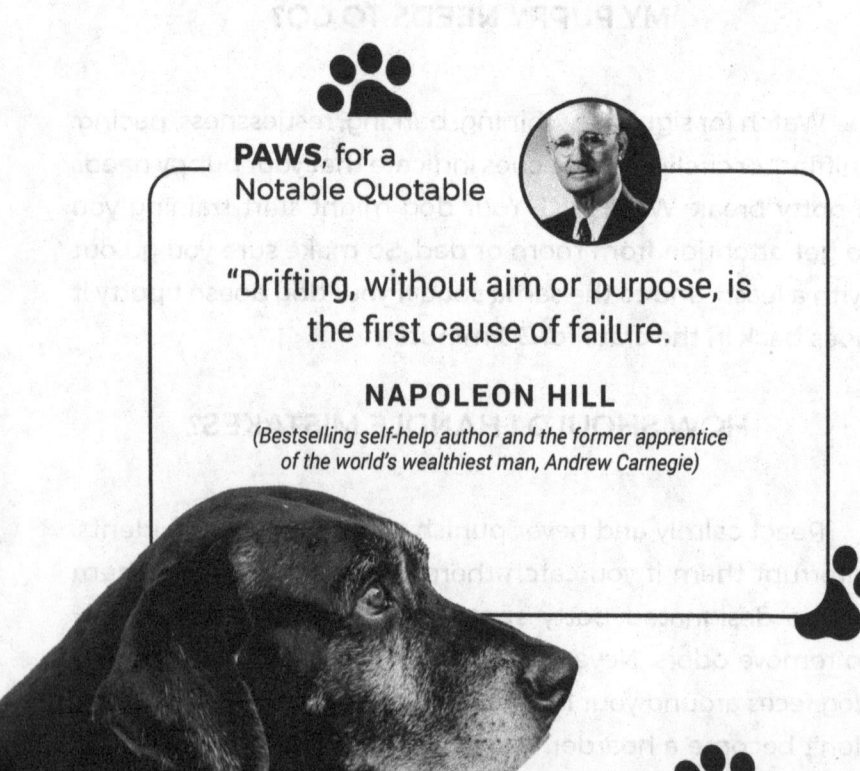

PAWS, for a
Notable Quotable

"Drifting, without aim or purpose, is the first cause of failure.

NAPOLEON HILL

(Bestselling self-help author and the former apprentice of the world's wealthiest man, Andrew Carnegie)

CHAPTER 13:

The Path to Promotion & Becoming the Perfect Employee

The path to promotion at Make Your Dog Epic Dog Training is not complicated, yet it does require hard work and diligence (the consistent application of effort).

Dependability - Dependability is the number one ability that we look for in the employees that we hire and promote into key leadership positions. As of the time that I am writing this I have been self-employed for 28 consecutive years and I have never taken a "sick day." I have never ghosted my employer because it's my birthday and I don't take off the Monday, Tuesday and Wednesday before Thanksgiving and the week of Christmas. Why? Because nothing works unless I do and we do. When a customer decides to entrust us with the training of their dog we must deliver results. Because if we do not WOW our customers they can simply fire us by taking their hard-earned money somewhere else.

PAWS, for a Notable Quotable

"You cannot control what happens to you, but you can control your attitude toward what happens to you, and in that, you will be mastering change rather than allowing it to master you."

BRIAN TRACY
(Legendary self-help author, business trainer, business mentor and business growth consultant)

Energy - If you decide to own a Make Your Dog Epic Dog Training location, know you need you to bring great energy every day, not weird energy. As of the time I am writing this, I went to bed last night at 9 PM and I woke up today at 3 AM. Why? That is my routine and that is how I have created the time needed to create several successful organizations while helping to raise 5 incredible kids, 4 goats, dozens of chickens, 11 cats and 1 dog (by the name of "Davis"). You need to do whatever you need to do before you get to work every day to bring GREAT ENERGY, CONTAGIOUS ENERGY and POSITIVE ENERGY to the workplace. No moping, no yawning, and no slacking. You must bring great ENERGY every day.

PAWS, for a
Notable Quotable

"Render more service than you are paid for and eventually you will be paid more for less services rendered."

NAPOLEON HILL

(The best-selling self-help author of all-time whose books have been constantly quoted by the world's most successful people.)

Energize - You must work to energize the dogs you are training and the people we are working with. It's your job to help create an environment of enthusiasm and if the person next to you is moping it's your job to pull the weeds of negativity and to sew the seeds of positivity immediately. You don't want to promote someone to a management position who does not have the ability to energize themselves and others.

PAWS, for a
Notable Quotable

"If you pick the right people and give them the opportunity to spread their wings and put compensation as a carrier behind it you almost don't have to manage them."

JACK WELCH
(The former CEO of GE who grew the company by 4,000% during his tenure)

Execute - You must learn how to effectively train dogs and you must carry a to-do-list and clipboard at all times if you want to be successful. It's very difficult to follow a checklist or remember what tasks you are supposed to do if you do not have them easily accessible and in front of you at all times. The pen is for remembering and the mind is for thinking. We can never become so busy that we forget to execute proven processes and best-practice systems. If you have the best attitude in the world it will not matter if you cannot train dogs or do your job effectively. Our company has been designed to be repeatable by our locations and clients, which is why our service is one of the most affordable services in the nation. However, our systems quickly become unrepeatable and unaffordable if everyone is not implementing best-practice systems.

Edge - You must be able to make the tough call and to do hard things. When you walk by a piece of trash at the office and no one else is around, do you pick it up? When you catch another employee engaging in a nefarious activity will you let your manager know. Having been self-employed and having mentored literally thousands of business owners, I can tell you patterns that I often see in cowardly, weak and

PAWS, for a
Notable Quotable

"Good checklists, on the other hand, are precise. They are efficient, to the point, and easy to use even in the most difficult situations. They do not try to spell out everything—a checklist cannot fly a plane. Instead, they provide reminders of only the most critical and important steps— the ones that even the highly skilled professionals using them could miss. Good checklists are, above all, practical."

ATUL GAWANDE

(Best-selling author of Checklist Manifesto and an American surgeon, writer and public speaker. He also has worked at the Harvard Medical School as their Professor of Surgery)

feeble-minded people. Weak people love to become keyboard warriors and to type things that they would never say to your face. Weak people love to embezzle money (embezzlement takes place when a person intentionally uses funds for a different purpose that they were intended to be used for, such as taking money from their business partner to enrich themselves, paying themselves $80,000 + to market their services to themselves, dramatically reducing the amount of money they are paying their partner without discussing it first and without having the legal authority to do so). Weak people love to avoid eye contact and prefer to communicate via text message and email. Weak people love to do the wrong thing in a quiet way for their own financial benefit. When you work at Make Your Dog Epic you must do unto others as you would have them do until you.

"Therefore all things whatsoever ye would that men should do to you, do ye even so to them: for this is the law and the prophets."

MATTHEW 7:12
(From The Bible)

Passion - You must have a passion for life and it must show up in the workplace and in all you do. If you want to become a Make Your Dog Epic Dog Training business owner YOU CAN DO IT! All you have to do is prove yourself as the best employee and teammate you can possibly be and you are on the path to success.

PAWS, for a
Notable Quotable

"Remembering that you are going to die is the best way I know to avoid the trap of thinking you have something to lose. You are already naked. There is no reason not to follow your heart."

STEVE JOBS

(The co-founder of Apple, the founder of NeXT and the former CEO of PIXAR)

What Does One Need to Do to Become Promoted At Make Your Dog Epic Dog Training?

🐾 **Step 1 - Show up to work on time and early every day.**

🐾 **Step 2 - Beat your boss work every day (if you want to get promoted really quickly)**

🐾 **Step 3 - Work accurately throughout the day while bringing positive energy and being honest.**

🐾 **Step 4 - Don't leave work until the job is done.**

CHAPTER 14:

Would You Like to Own a Make Your Dog Epic Business & Location?

(A SPECIAL MESSAGE FROM CLAY CLARK)

Are you looking for a business vehicle that you can start quickly and requires minimal startup cost? Are you looking to earn extra income? Have you ever thought of opening your own business? Have you ever thought of opening a business, but you couldn't quite figure out the right business niche, products and services to offer? Are you tired of working in politically correct corporate America? If you earned both time and financial freedom what would you do with your extra time and income? If you are interested in a Make Your Dog Epic location ownership, reach out to us at www.MakeYourDogEpic.com/contact.

PAWS, for a Notable Quotable

"The secret of happiness is minimizing the amount of time you spend with people you don't choose to be with. This is just math!"

PHIL LIBIN
(The Co-founder of Evernote)

Want to open your own Make Your Dog Epic dog training business? Learn how to have your own epic adventure by opening one of the most affordable and turn-key dog training businesses on the planet!

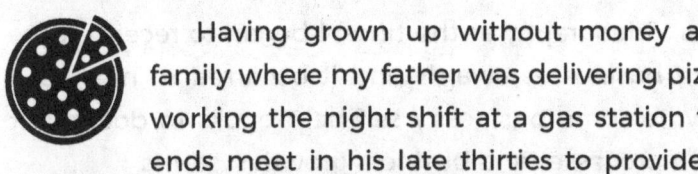 Having grown up without money and in a family where my father was delivering pizzas and working the night shift at a gas station to make ends meet in his late thirties to provide for our family despite having a college degree, I know what it's like to start with nothing and to build a successful, scalable and turn-key business model. I started my first business out of my parent's Cokato, Minnesota basement at the age of 15 (www.DJConnection.com). I know what it's like to work at three jobs simultaneously (Applebee's, Target & DirecTV) in order to save up enough money to get my entertainment business and bridal expo / wedding show business off the ground.

I know what it is like to actually work 119 hours per week (which is 17 Hours per day) in order to build a successful business that is capable of producing both financial and time freedom for my family and I. I love entrepreneurship! I love finding a problem, solving it, creating a win-win price point for businesses and customers and scaling it and that is a big reason why I love dog training!!! I love creating jobs for wonderful people like you to transform their dog from a terrorist into their best friend and I love creating jobs for our wonderful employees who love to deliver their training skills with a spirit of excellence.

Since the age of 15, I have not stopped starting, growing and scaling successful businesses because I enjoy it, I'm good at it and it is what I have learned how to master in these last 29 years of being self-employed. Around the age of 25, after I had started and grown several successful companies including: www.DJConnection.com, The Tulsa Wedding Show, a videography company (which was known as Cherished

Traditions Videography at the time) I began to receive more and more businesses awards and it occurred to me that I should write some business / self-help books to document my proven processes and business growth systems.

After writing those books, MASSIVE companies like UPS, Hewlett Packard, O'Reilly Auto Parts, QuikTrip, Boeing, Bama Companies and colleges kept asking me to educate, to inspire and to teach their groups how to start and grow a successful business. However, after having delivered well over 300 keynote presentations I discovered that audiences enjoyed my training and workshops, but they found it to be impossible to really learn how to build successful business systems and scalable businesses without on-going weekly mentorship, training and accountability.

PAWS, for a
Notable Quotable

"The time will never be just right, you must act now."

NAPOLEON HILL

(The best-selling author of Think & Grow Rich, the book that changed my life. Napoleon Hill's writings had such a huge impact on me that I actually named my son Aubrey Napoleon-Hill Clark after Napoleon Hill in honor of the positive and life-changing impact that his writings had on my life).

Having helped thousands of entrepreneurs to turn their business ideas into successful companies I've discovered that teaching someone to grow successful companies requires on-going weekly mentorship and accountability so that you don't begin to lose focus and drift over time. That is why I started coaching clients on a weekly and on-going basis. The results that we have been able to produce for our clients has been life-changing for them (and you can watch thousands of real-life client success stories at www.ThrivetimeShow.com).

If you decide to join the Make Your Dog Epic family, you will have the opportunity for my team and I to essentially mentor you, coach you, and hold you accountable on a weekly basis. We want your business to Thrive.

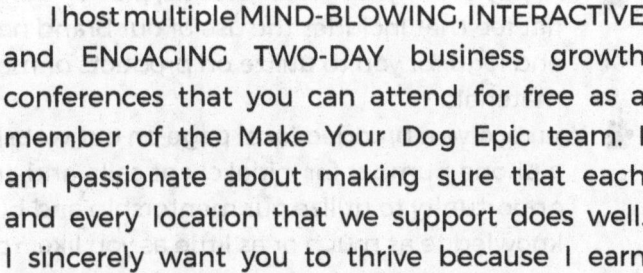

I host multiple MIND-BLOWING, INTERACTIVE and ENGAGING TWO-DAY business growth conferences that you can attend for free as a member of the Make Your Dog Epic team. I am passionate about making sure that each and every location that we support does well. I sincerely want you to thrive because I earn revenue for helping you, mentoring you, guiding you down the path, and assisting with online advertising. We offer each and every location with the weekly business growth coaching, consulting, mentoring and accountability, to ensure nobody drifts to success. It is up to you how much of our assets you take advantage of.

HOW MUCH DOES IT COST TO OPEN A MAKE YOUR DOG EPIC DOG TRAINING BUSINESS?

- 🐾 You must have a dog that will serve as your best friend and demonstration dog for customers.
- 🐾 You must have a vehicle to safely transport dogs.
- 🐾 You must supply a safe and climate controlled location for the training of dogs.
- 🐾 You must we a use a dog training technique that utilizes industry best-practices and includes positive reinforcement that we refer to as: focus-based, positive reinforcement training and methodology.
- 🐾 We include a program for the weekly on-going mentorship, training, coaching, online advertisement management, website maintenance, search engine optimization, etc. for you to access at your will.
- 🐾 You pay 6% of your gross revenue, plus a 750/month flat fee that includes the use of our brand name and logo for you to utilize on products or marketing materials.
- 🐾 You receive a branded local page on our website, a phone number for initial client calls, and an opportunity to utilize our mentorship and business knowledge as much or as little as you like. You set prices, packages, control on-going appointments, and control employee wages.
- 🐾 We require you to use whatever best-practice training techniques you are most comfortable with and have produced great results for you while training dogs. We only require you to incorporate positive reinforcement training into your routine. We do not consider the use of shock collars as a best-practice training technique. Some trainers prefer the use of e-collars while others use clicker training and others positive reinforcement only. That is up to you.

Want to open your own Make Your Dog Epic dog training business?
Learn how to have your own epic adventure by opening one of the
most affordable and turn-key dog training businesses on the planet!

WHAT WILL YOUR WEEKLY SCHEDULE LOOK LIKE AS A MAKE YOUR DOG EPIC BUSINESS OWNER?

- 🐾 You train dogs.

- 🐾 You train people to train dogs.

- 🐾 You interview people to hire to train dogs.

Listed on the additional pages below you will find countless success stories of real-life clients that we have really helped.

PAWS, for a Notable Quotable

"Without a plan for your life, it is easier to follow the course of least resistance, to go with the flow, to drift with the current with no particular destination in mind. Having a definite plan for your life greatly simplifies the process of making hundreds of daily decisions that affect your ultimate success. When you know where you want to go, you can quickly decide if your actions are moving you toward your goal or away from it. Without definite, precise goals and a plan for their achievement, each decision must be considered in a vacuum. Definiteness of purpose provides context and allows you to relate specific actions to your overall plan."

NAPOLEON HILL

(The best-selling author of Think & Grow Rich, the book that changed my life. Napoleon Hill's writings had such a huge impact on me that I actually named my son Aubrey Napoleon-Hill Clark after Napoleon Hill in honor of the positive and life-changing impact that his writings had on my life).

Want to open your own Make Your Dog Epic dog training business?
Learn how to have your own epic adventure by opening one of the most affordable and turn-key dog training businesses on the planet!

Interested in owning
your own business?

Learn more about
how to open your
very own

Make Your
Dog Epic

business location
today at:

www.MakeYourDogEpic.com

See thousands of real Clay Clark success
stories, case studies, and client testimonials
today at www.ThrivetimeShow.com

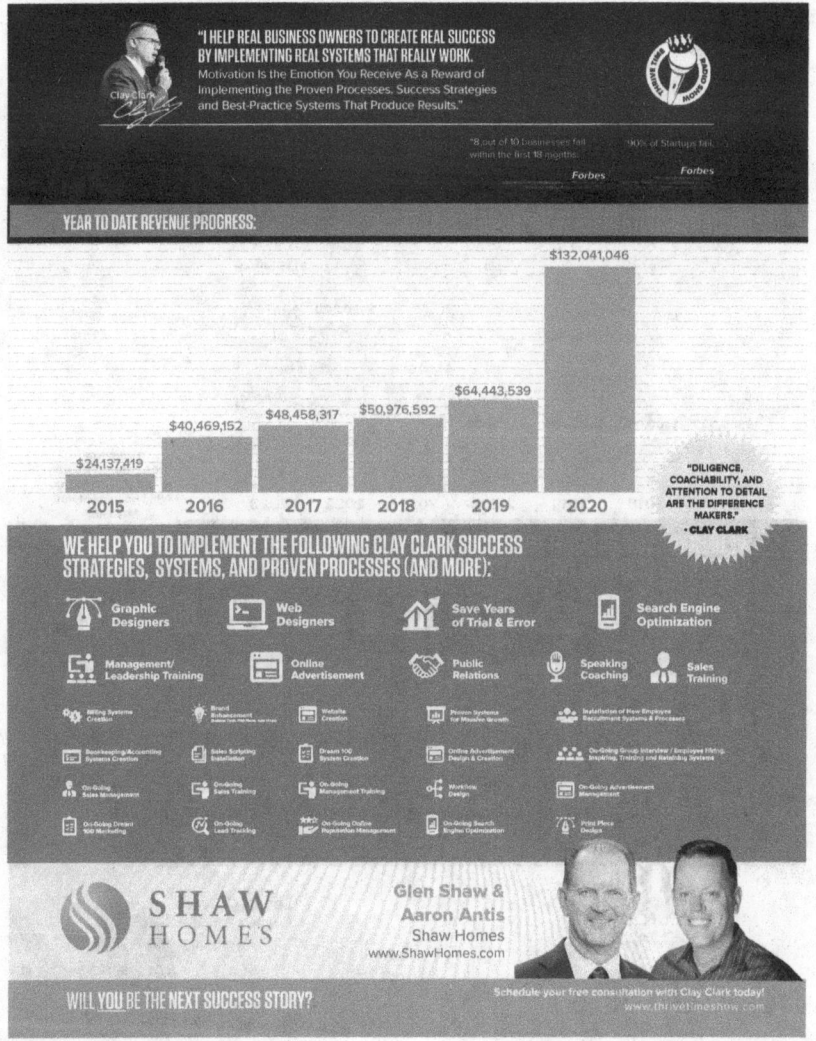

See thousands of real Clay Clark success stories, case studies, and client testimonials today at www.ThrivetimeShow.com

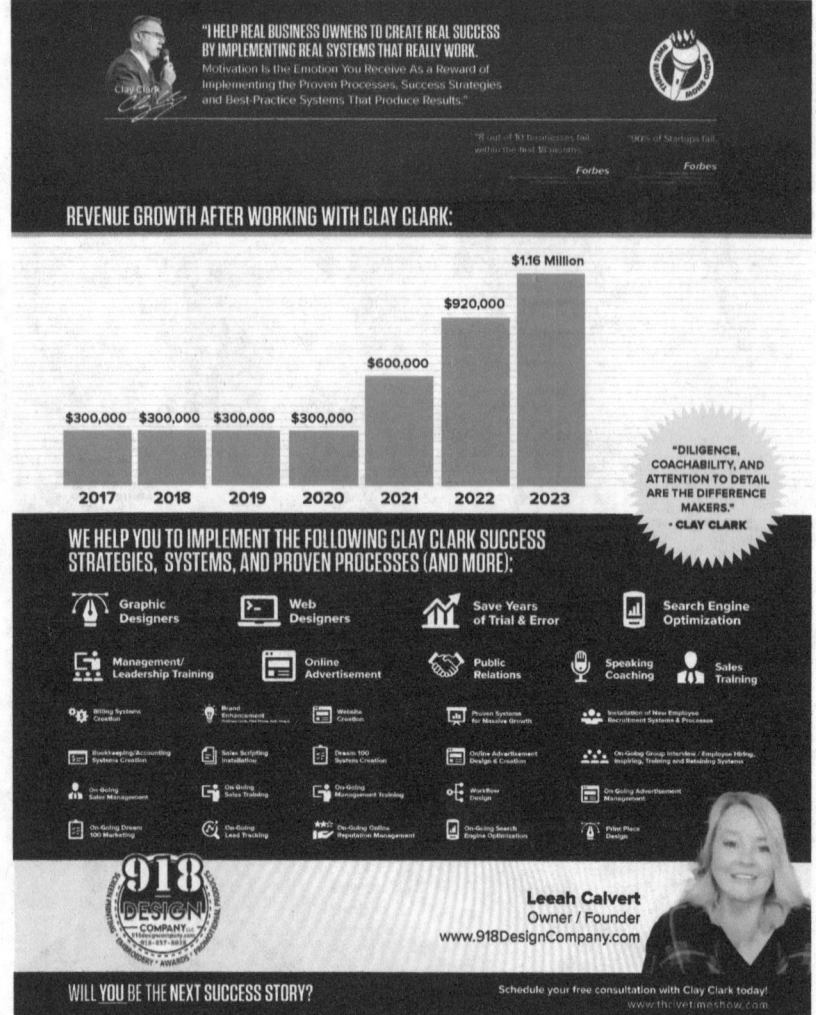

See thousands of real Clay Clark success stories, case studies, and client testimonials today at www.ThrivetimeShow.com

See thousands of real Clay Clark success stories, case studies, and client testimonials today at www.ThrivetimeShow.com

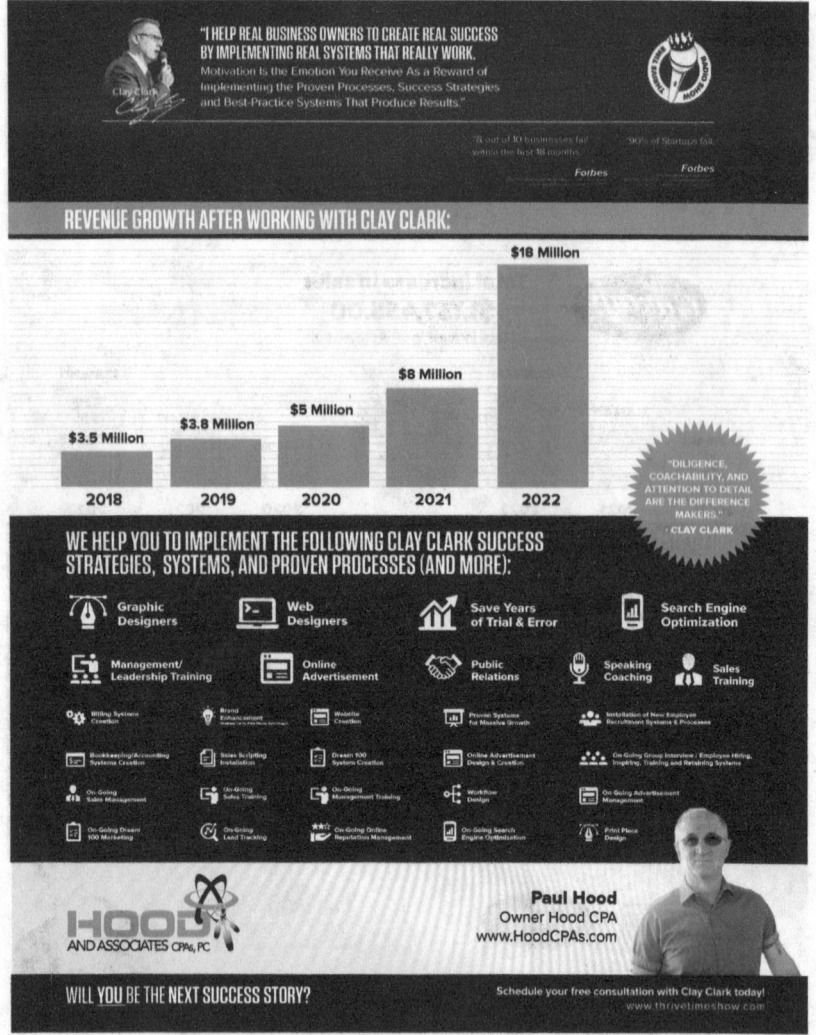

See thousands of real Clay Clark success stories, case studies, and client testimonials today at www.ThrivetimeShow.com

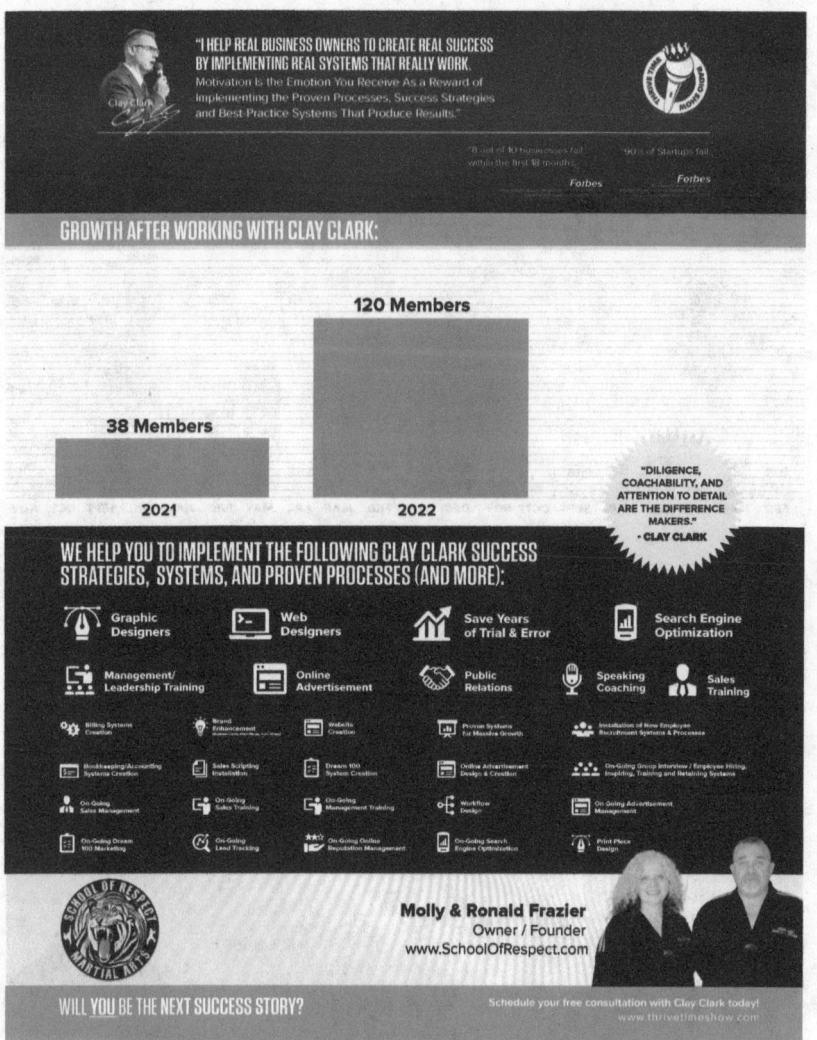

See thousands of real Clay Clark success stories, case studies, and client testimonials today at www.ThrivetimeShow.com

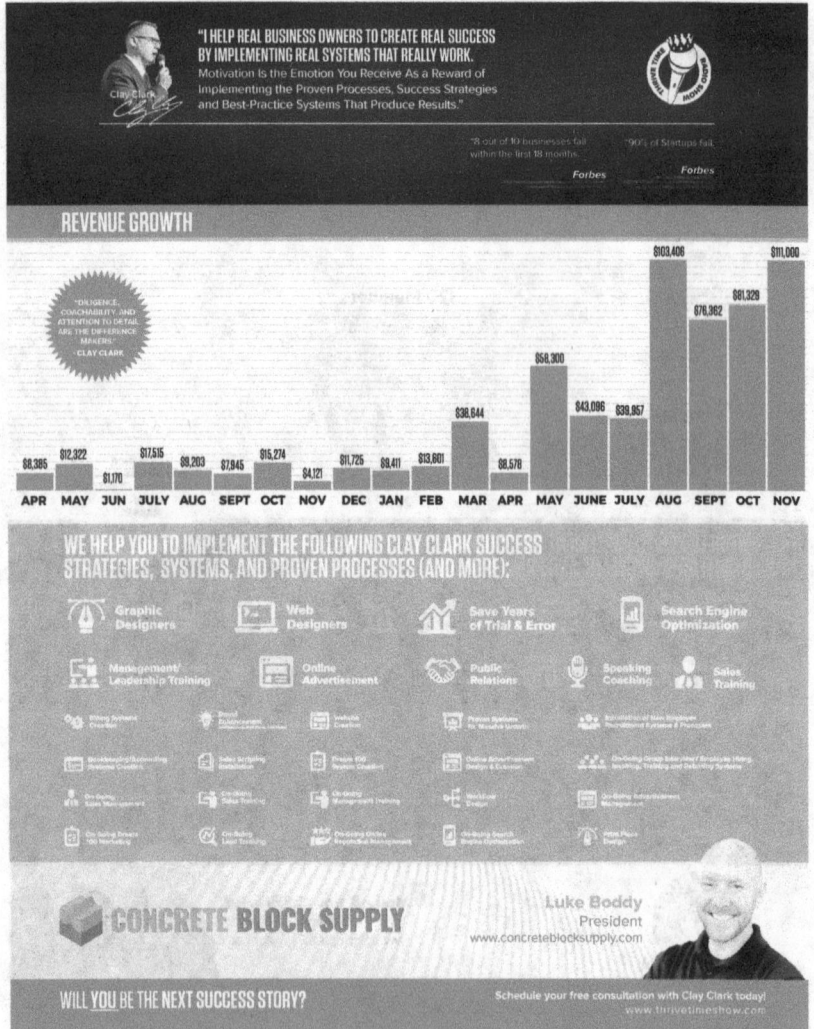

See thousands of real Clay Clark success stories, case studies, and client testimonials today at www.ThrivetimeShow.com

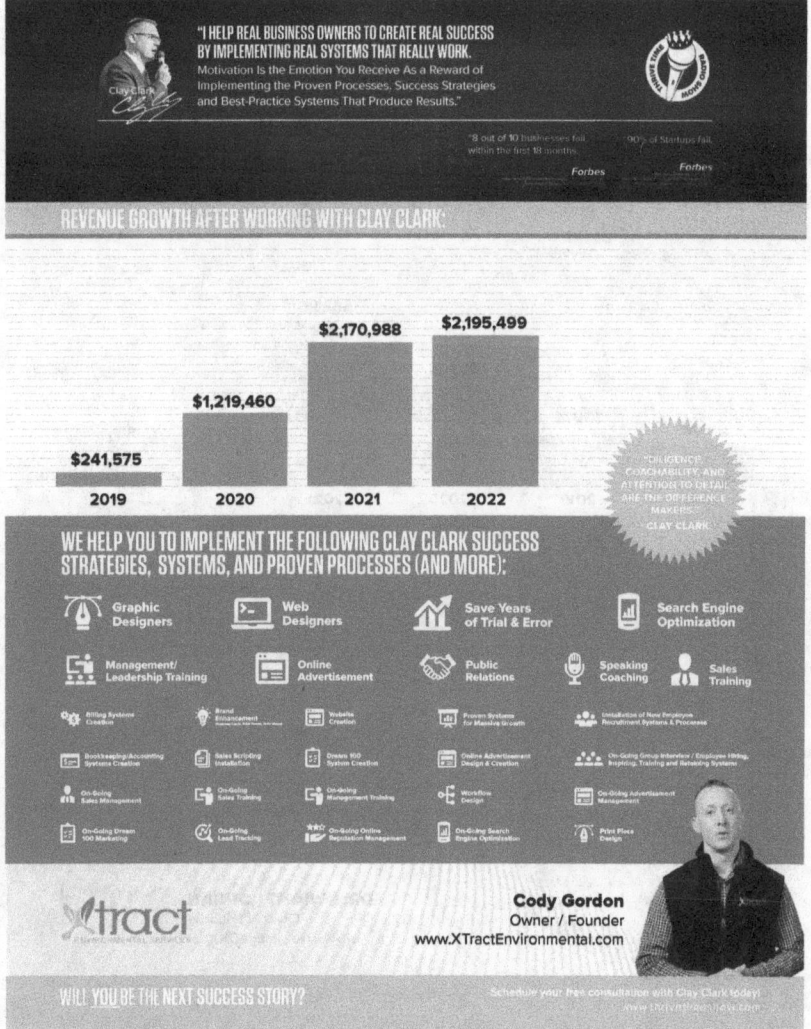

See thousands of real Clay Clark success stories, case studies, and client testimonials today at www.ThrivetimeShow.com

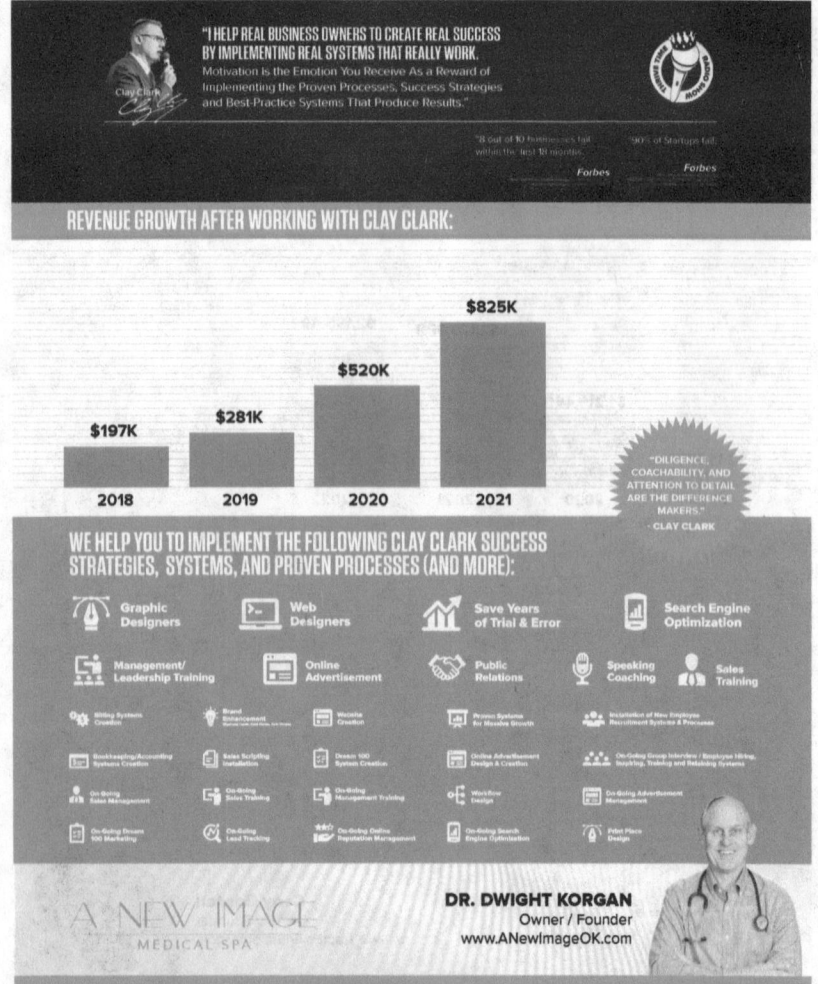

See thousands of real Clay Clark success stories, case studies, and client testimonials today at www.ThrivetimeShow.com

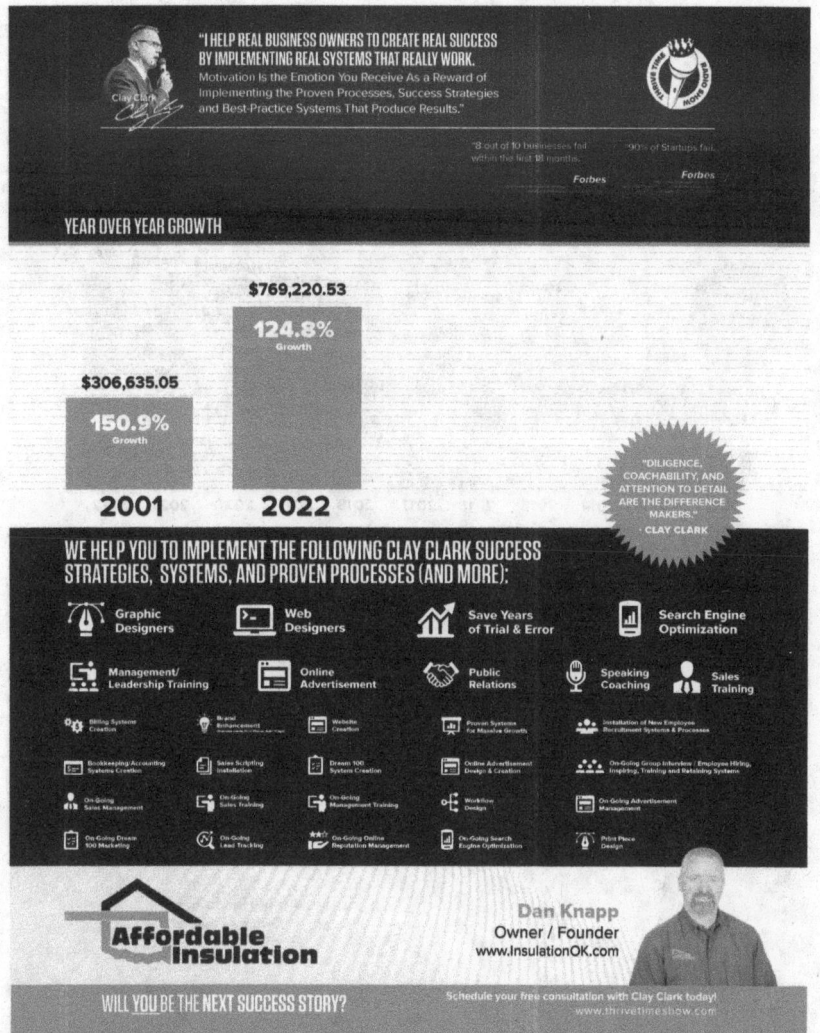

See thousands of real Clay Clark success stories, case studies, and client testimonials today at www.ThrivetimeShow.com

See thousands of real Clay Clark success stories, case studies, and client testimonials today at www.ThrivetimeShow.com

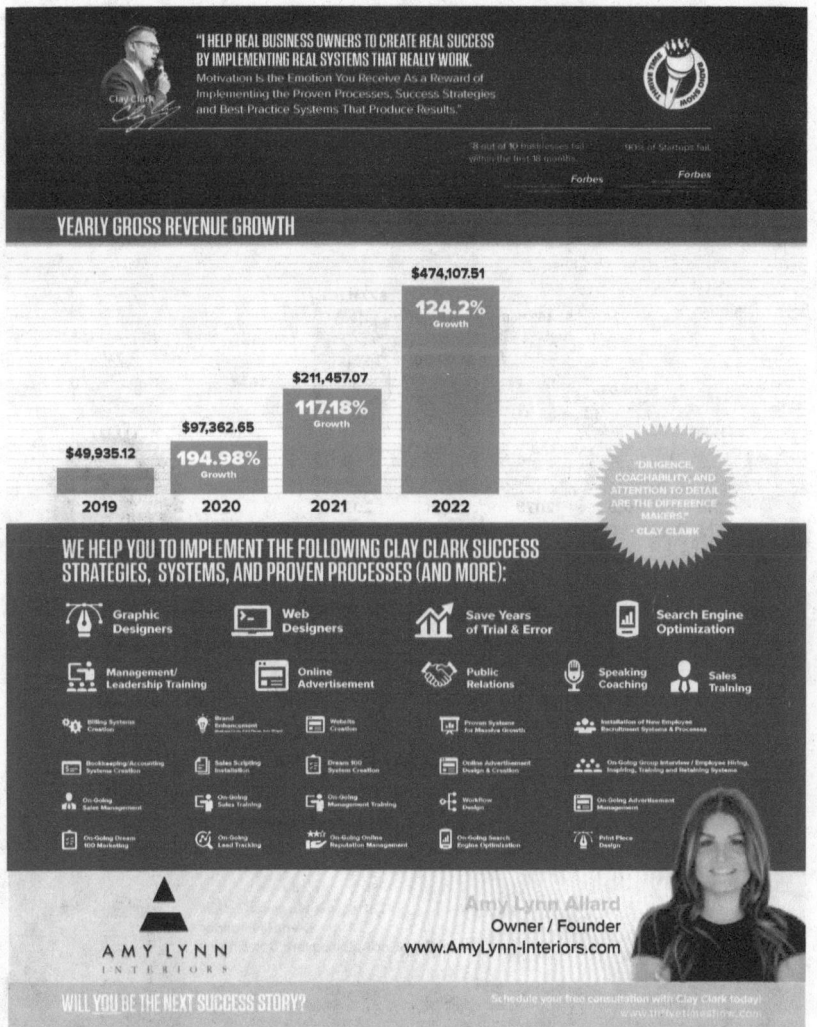

See thousands of real Clay Clark success stories, case studies, and client testimonials today at www.ThrivetimeShow.com

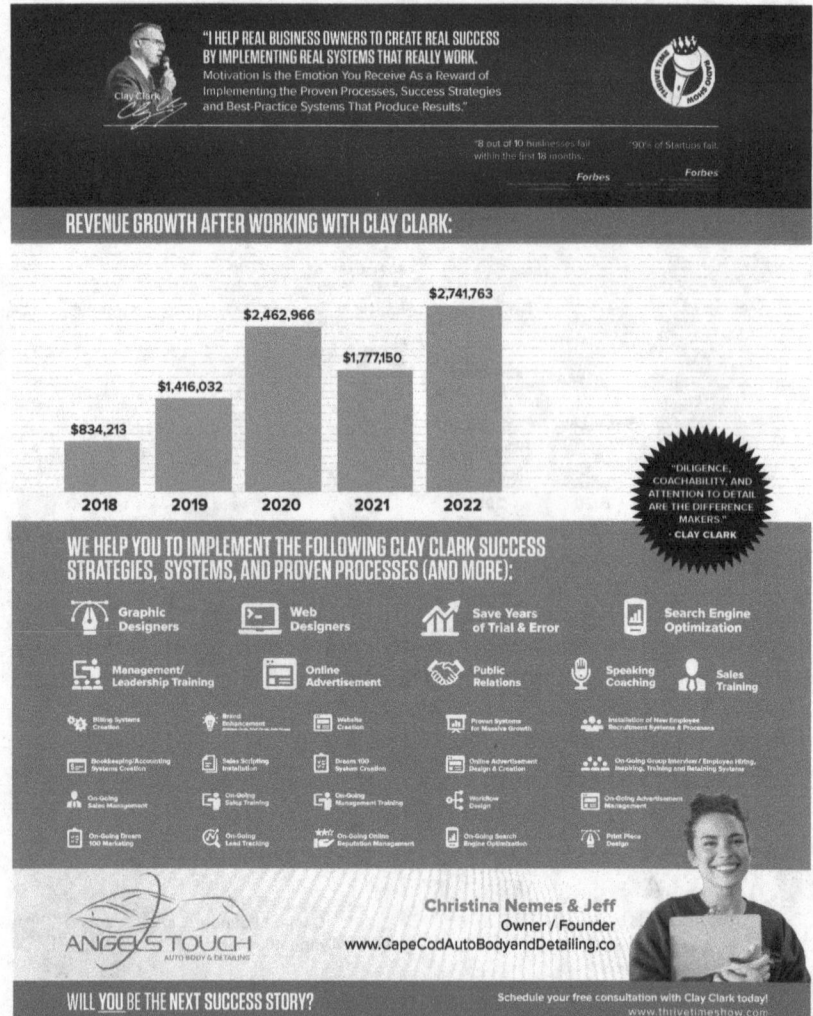

"I HELP REAL BUSINESS OWNERS TO CREATE REAL SUCCESS BY IMPLEMENTING REAL SYSTEMS THAT REALLY WORK. Motivation Is the Emotion You Receive As a Reward of Implementing the Proven Processes, Success Strategies and Best-Practice Systems That Produce Results."

Clay Clark

"8 out of 10 businesses fail within the first 18 months. — Forbes

"90% of Startups fail. — Forbes

REVENUE GROWTH AFTER WORKING WITH CLAY CLARK:

2018	2019	2020	2021	2022
$834,213	$1,416,032	$2,462,966	$1,777,150	$2,741,763

"DILIGENCE, COACHABILITY, AND ATTENTION TO DETAIL ARE THE DIFFERENCE MAKERS." - CLAY CLARK

WE HELP YOU TO IMPLEMENT THE FOLLOWING CLAY CLARK SUCCESS STRATEGIES, SYSTEMS, AND PROVEN PROCESSES (AND MORE):

- Graphic Designers
- Web Designers
- Save Years of Trial & Error
- Search Engine Optimization
- Management/ Leadership Training
- Online Advertisement
- Public Relations
- Speaking Coaching
- Sales Training
- Billing Systems Creation
- Brand Enhancement
- Website Creation
- Proven Systems for Massive Growth
- Installation of New Employee Recruitment Systems & Processes
- Bookkeeping/Accounting Systems Creation
- Sales Scripting Installation
- Dream 100 System Creation
- Online Advertisement Design & Creation
- On-Going Group Interview / Employee Hiring, Inspiring, Training and Retaining Systems
- On-Going Sales Management
- On-Going Sales Training
- On-Going Management Training
- Workflow Design
- On-Going Advertisement Management
- On-Going Dream 100 Marketing
- On-Going Lead Tracking
- On-Going Online Reputation Management
- On-Going Search Engine Optimization
- Print Piece Design

ANGELS TOUCH AUTO BODY & DETAILING

Christina Nemes & Jeff Owner / Founder www.CapeCodAutoBodyandDetailing.co

WILL **YOU** BE THE NEXT SUCCESS STORY?

Schedule your free consultation with Clay Clark today! www.thrivetimeshow.com

See thousands of real Clay Clark success stories, case studies, and client testimonials today at www.ThrivetimeShow.com

See thousands of real Clay Clark success stories, case studies, and client testimonials today at www.ThrivetimeShow.com

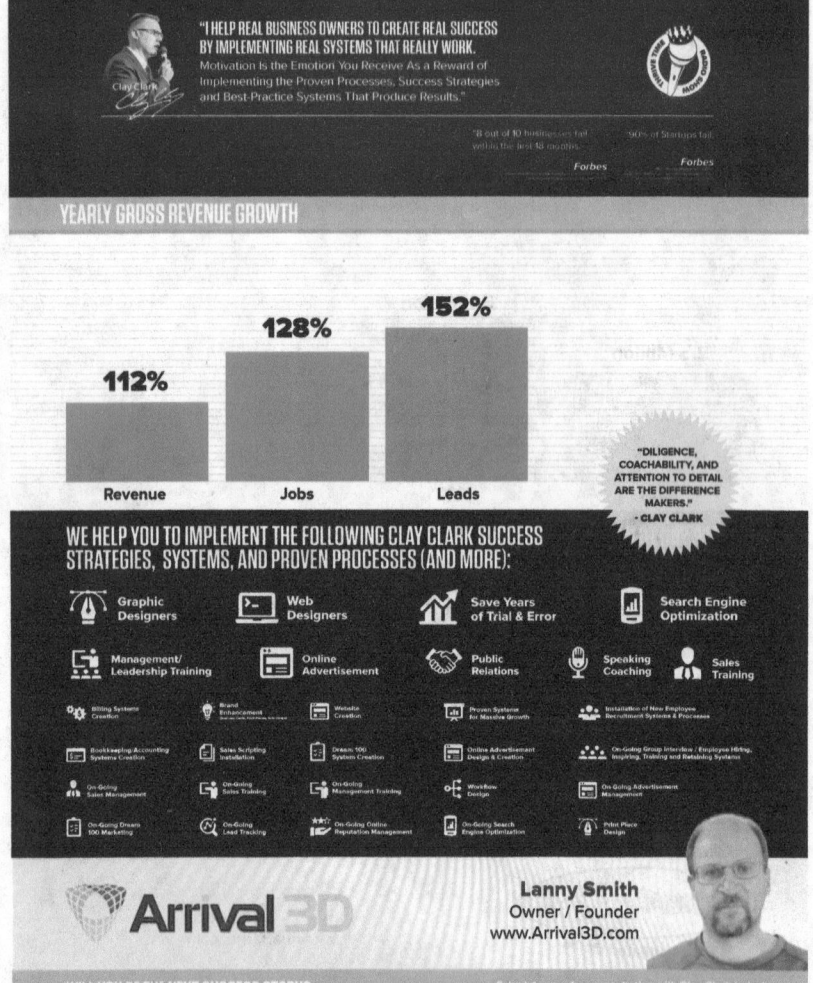

See thousands of real Clay Clark success stories, case studies, and client testimonials today at www.ThrivetimeShow.com

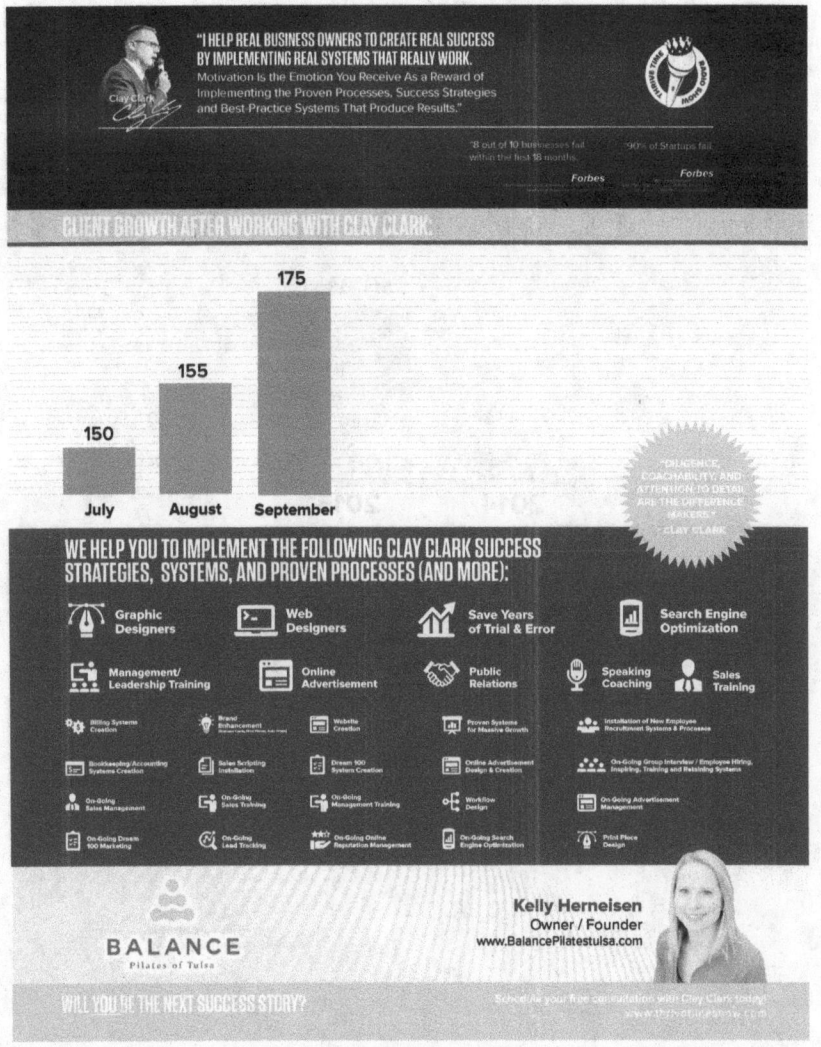

See thousands of real Clay Clark success stories, case studies, and client testimonials today at www.ThrivetimeShow.com

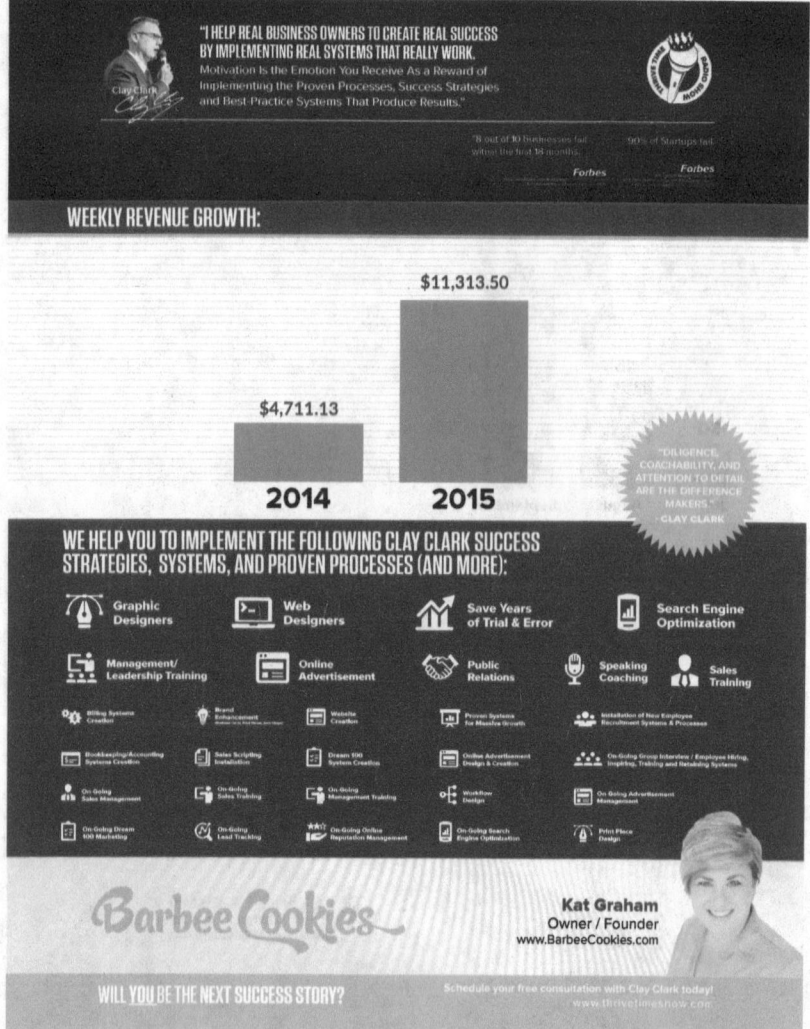

See thousands of real Clay Clark success stories, case studies, and client testimonials today at www.ThrivetimeShow.com

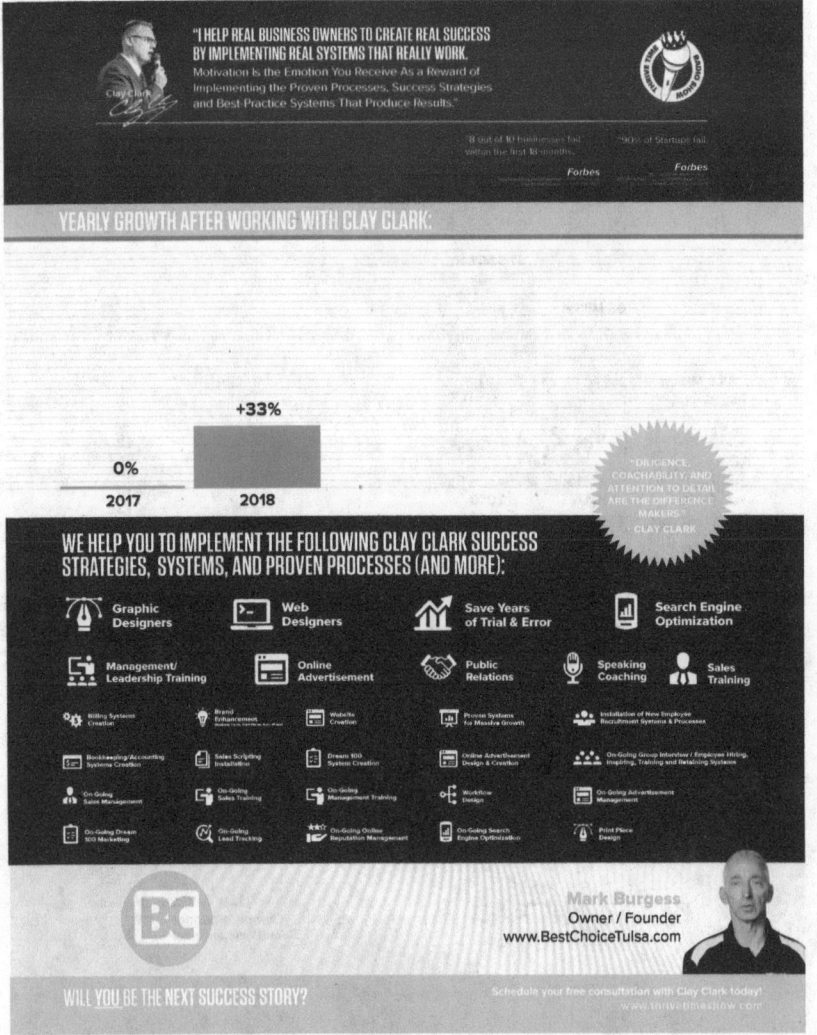

See thousands of real Clay Clark success stories, case studies, and client testimonials today at www.ThrivetimeShow.com

See thousands of real Clay Clark success stories, case studies, and client testimonials today at www.ThrivetimeShow.com

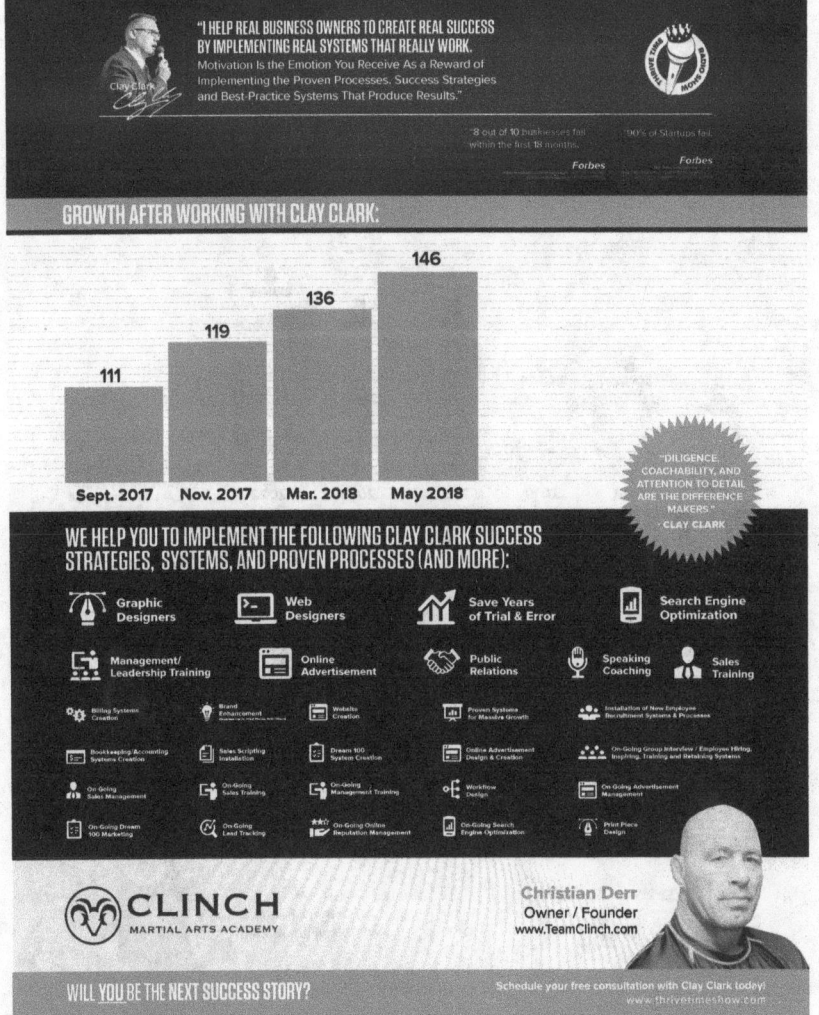

See thousands of real Clay Clark success stories, case studies, and client testimonials today at www.ThrivetimeShow.com

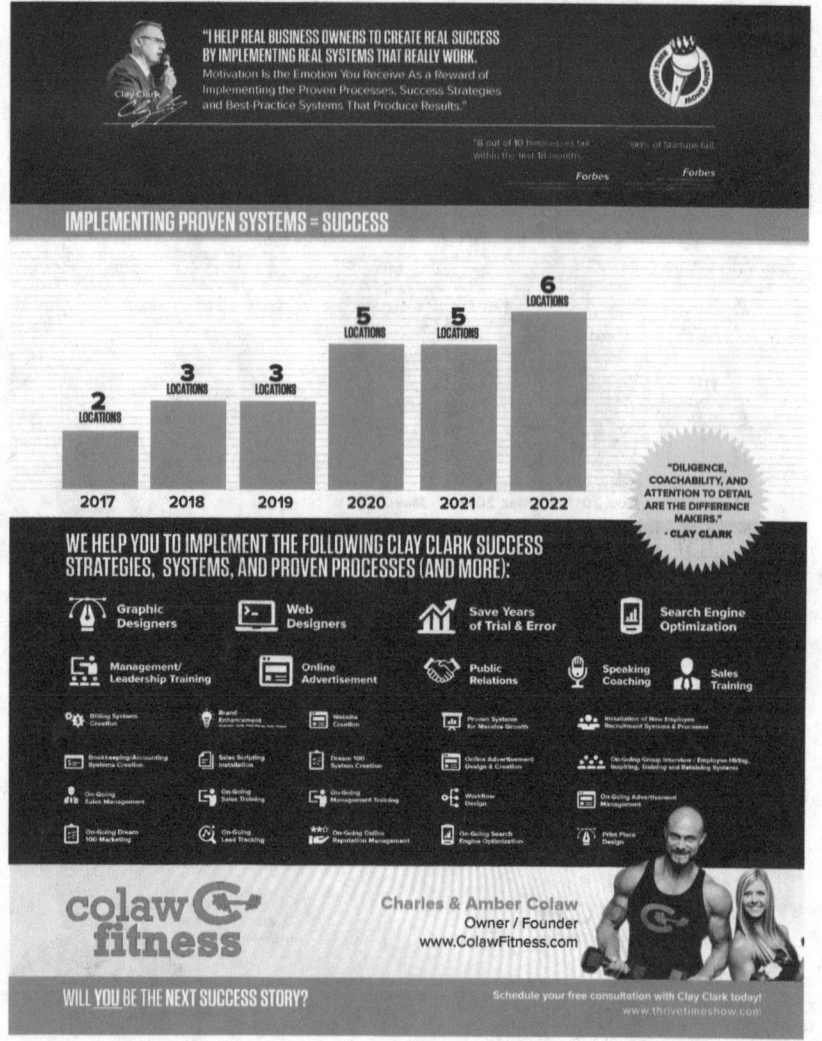

See thousands of real Clay Clark success stories, case studies, and client testimonials today at www.ThrivetimeShow.com

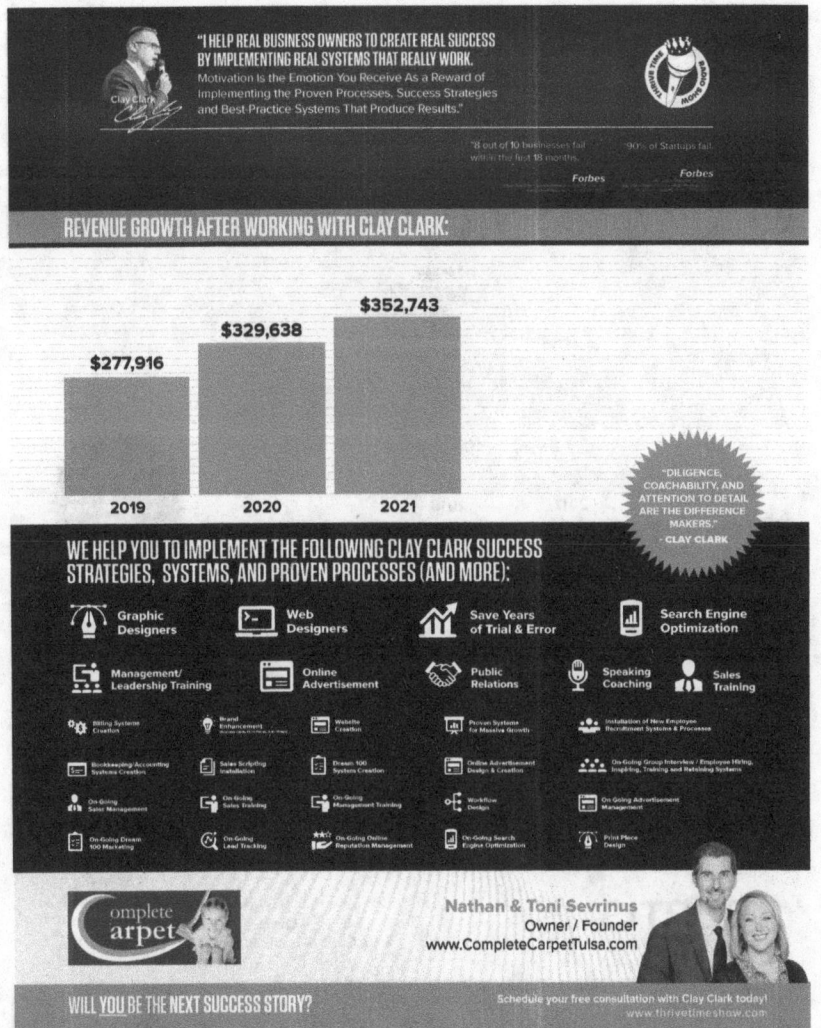

See thousands of real Clay Clark success stories, case studies, and client testimonials today at www.ThrivetimeShow.com

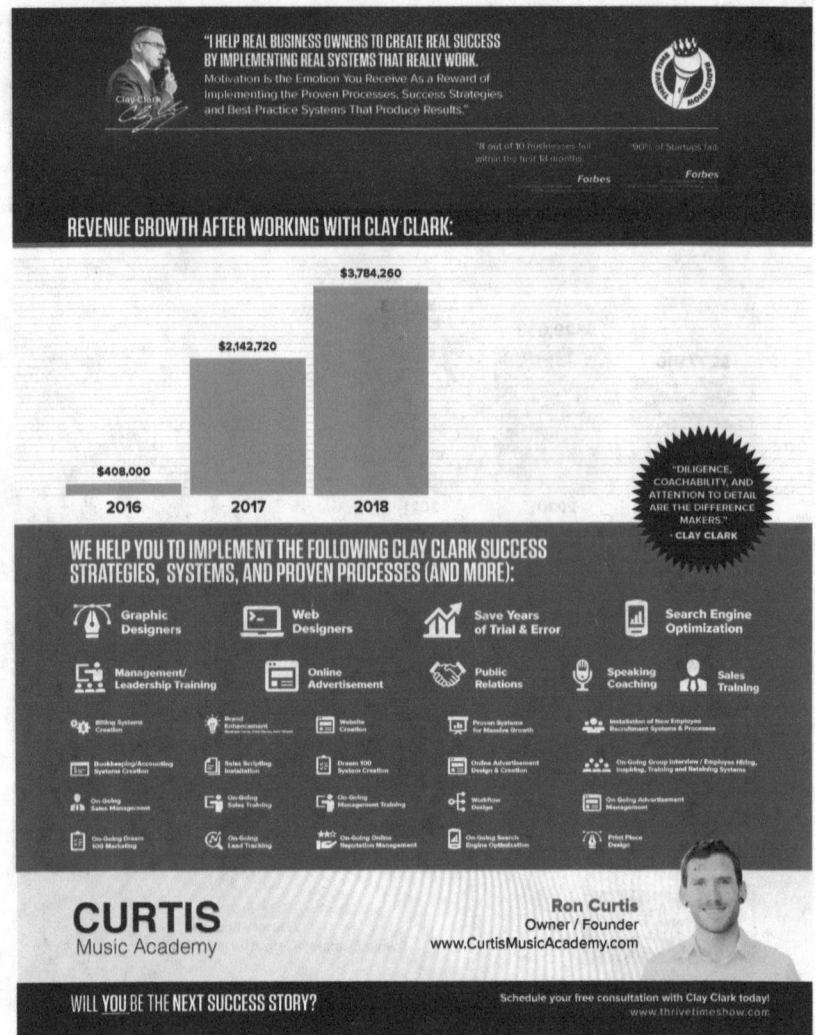

See thousands of real Clay Clark success stories, case studies, and client testimonials today at www.ThrivetimeShow.com

See thousands of real Clay Clark success stories, case studies, and client testimonials today at www.ThrivetimeShow.com

See thousands of real Clay Clark success
stories, case studies, and client testimonials
today at www.ThrivetimeShow.com

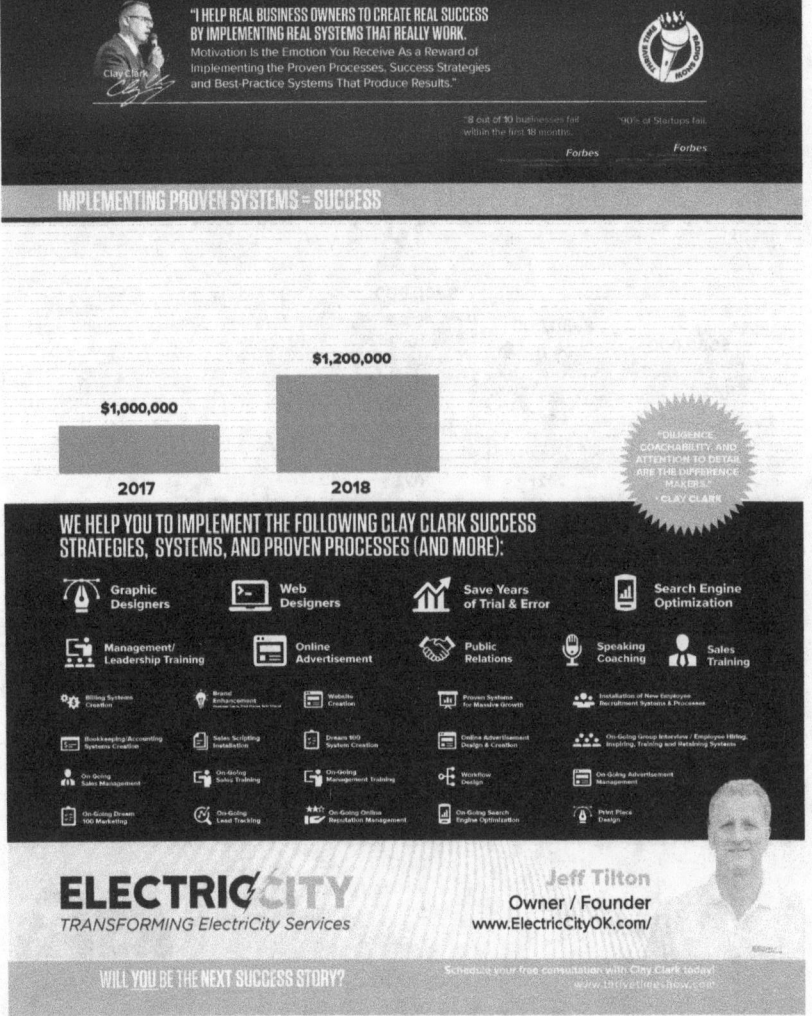

See thousands of real Clay Clark success stories, case studies, and client testimonials today at www.ThrivetimeShow.com

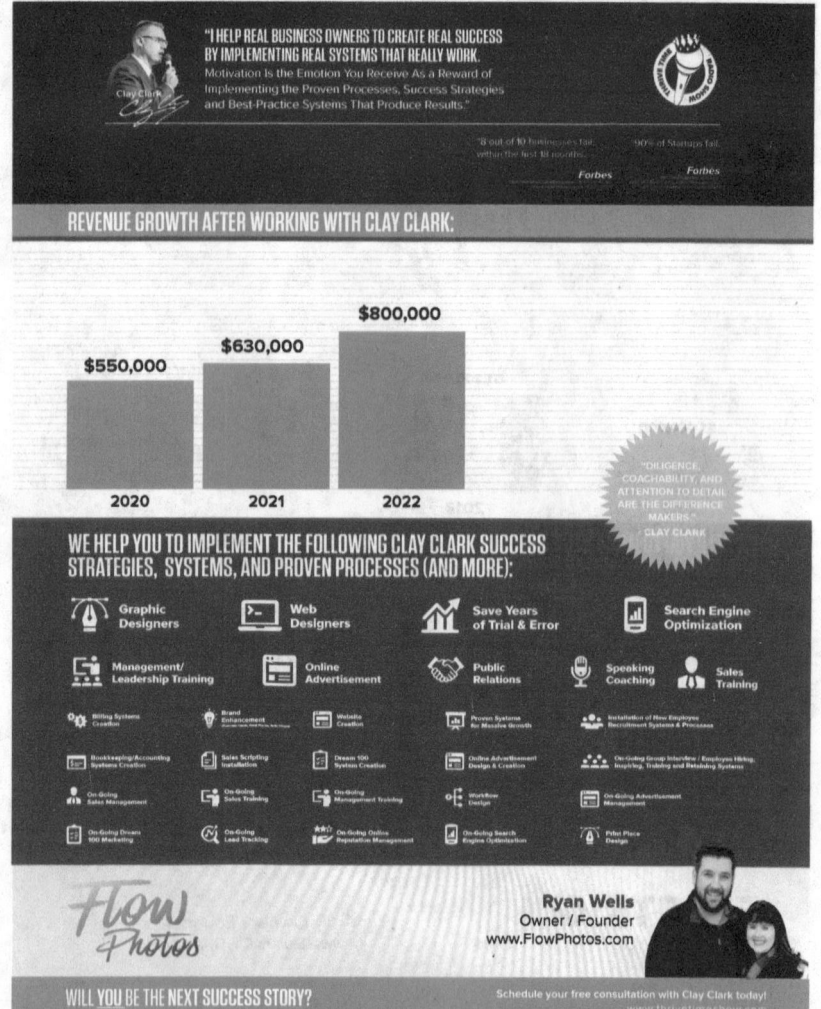

See thousands of real Clay Clark success stories, case studies, and client testimonials today at www.ThrivetimeShow.com

See thousands of real Clay Clark success stories, case studies, and client testimonials today at www.ThrivetimeShow.com

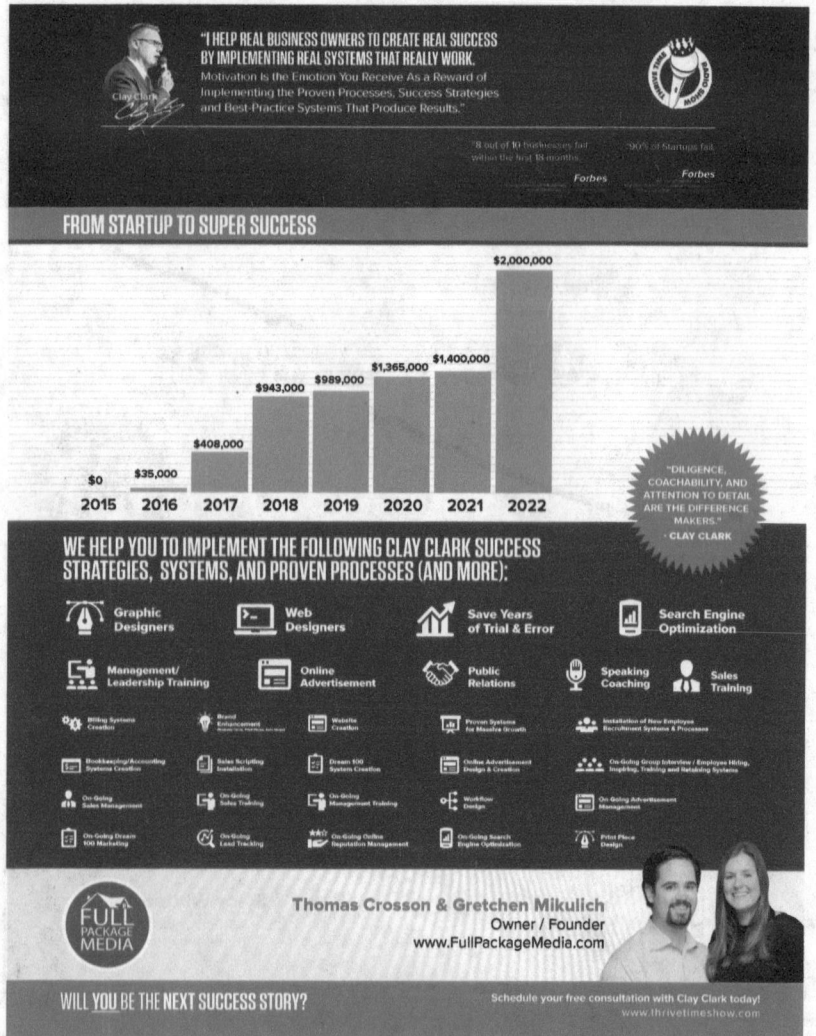

See thousands of real Clay Clark success stories, case studies, and client testimonials today at www.ThrivetimeShow.com

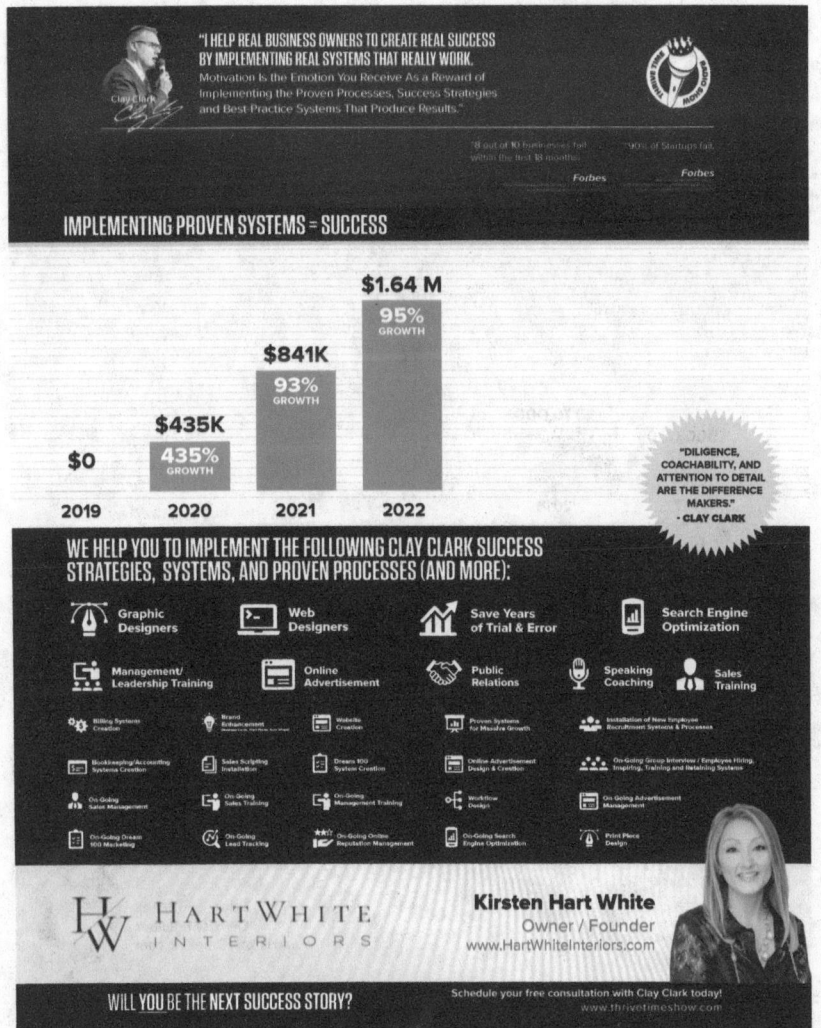

See thousands of real Clay Clark success stories, case studies, and client testimonials today at www.ThrivetimeShow.com

See thousands of real Clay Clark success stories, case studies, and client testimonials today at www.ThrivetimeShow.com

See thousands of real Clay Clark success stories, case studies, and client testimonials today at www.ThrivetimeShow.com

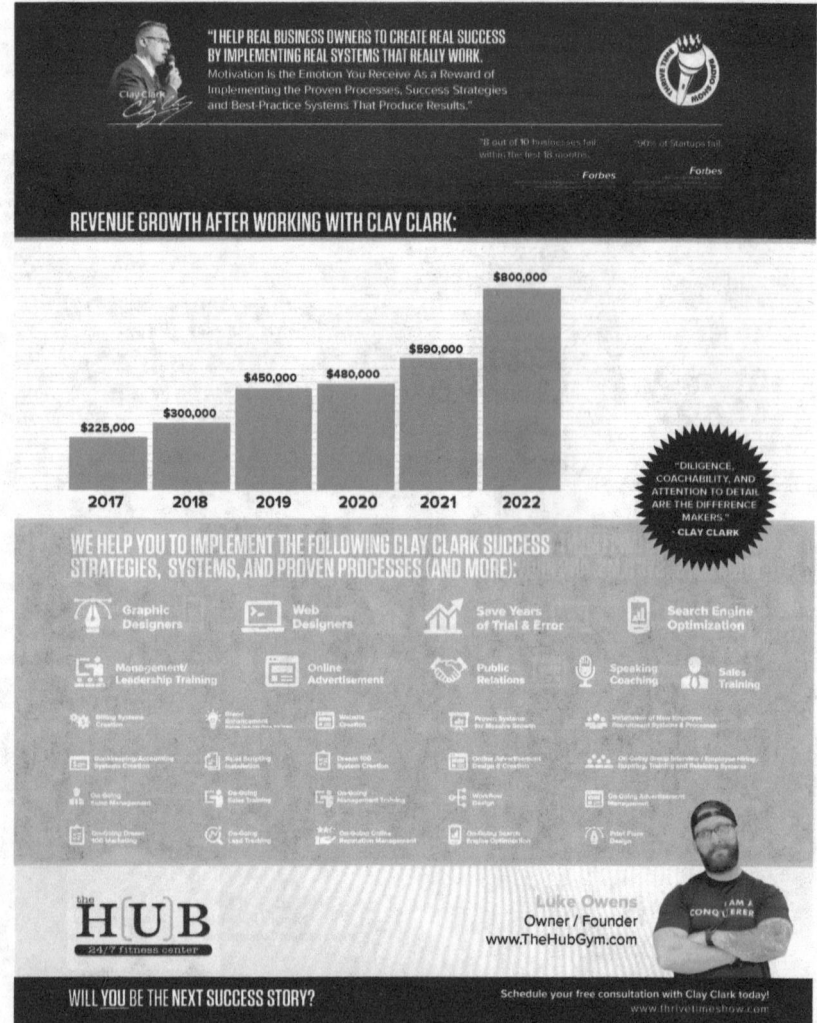

See thousands of real Clay Clark success stories, case studies, and client testimonials today at www.ThrivetimeShow.com

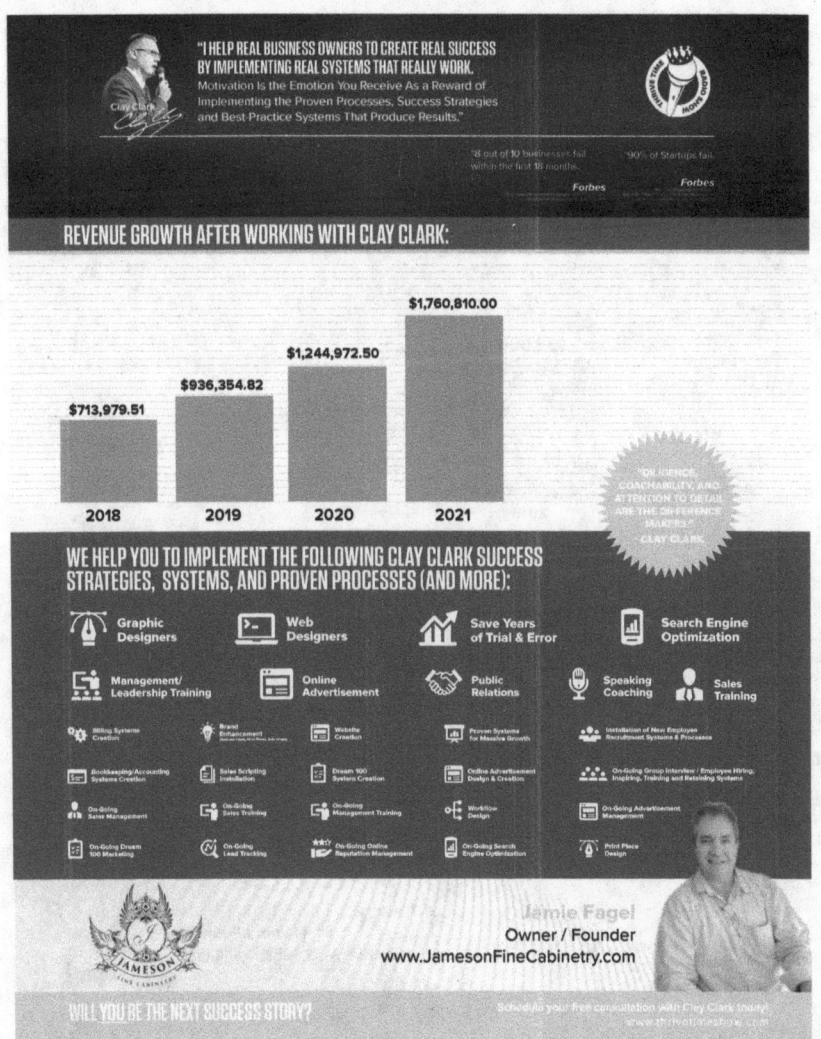

See thousands of real Clay Clark success stories, case studies, and client testimonials today at www.ThrivetimeShow.com

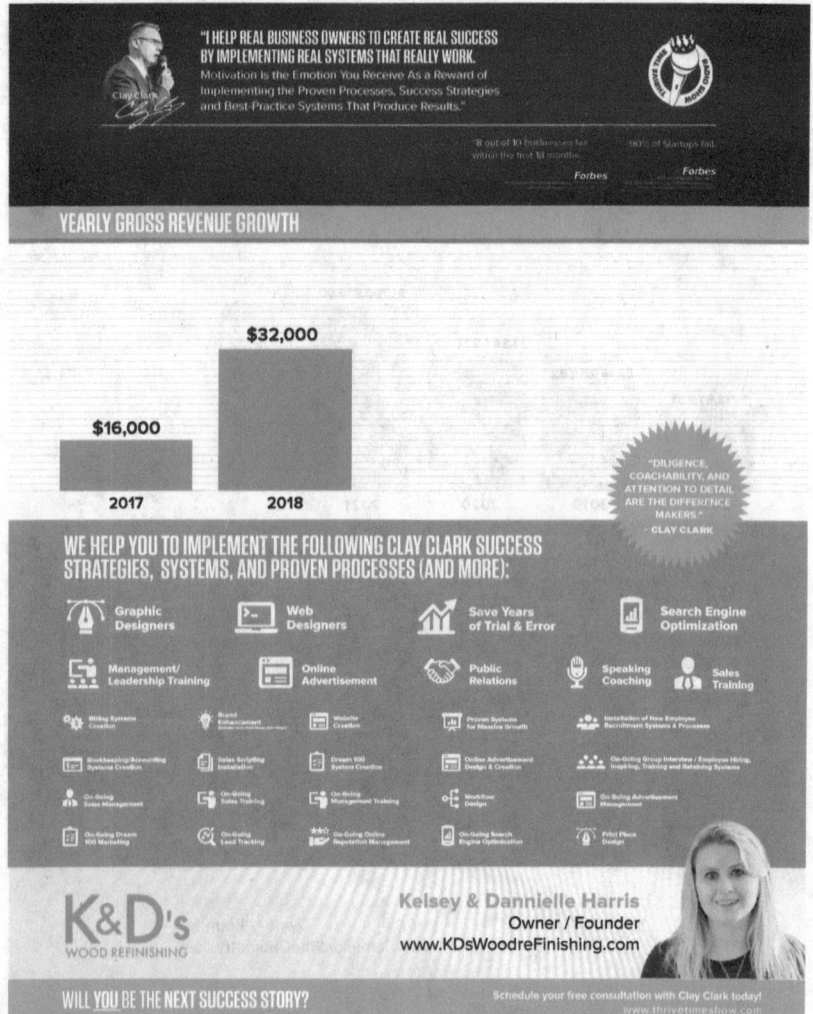
Want to open your own Make Your Dog Epic dog training business? Learn how to have your own epic adventure by opening one of the most affordable and turn-key dog training businesses on the planet!

See thousands of real Clay Clark success stories, case studies, and client testimonials today at www.ThrivetimeShow.com

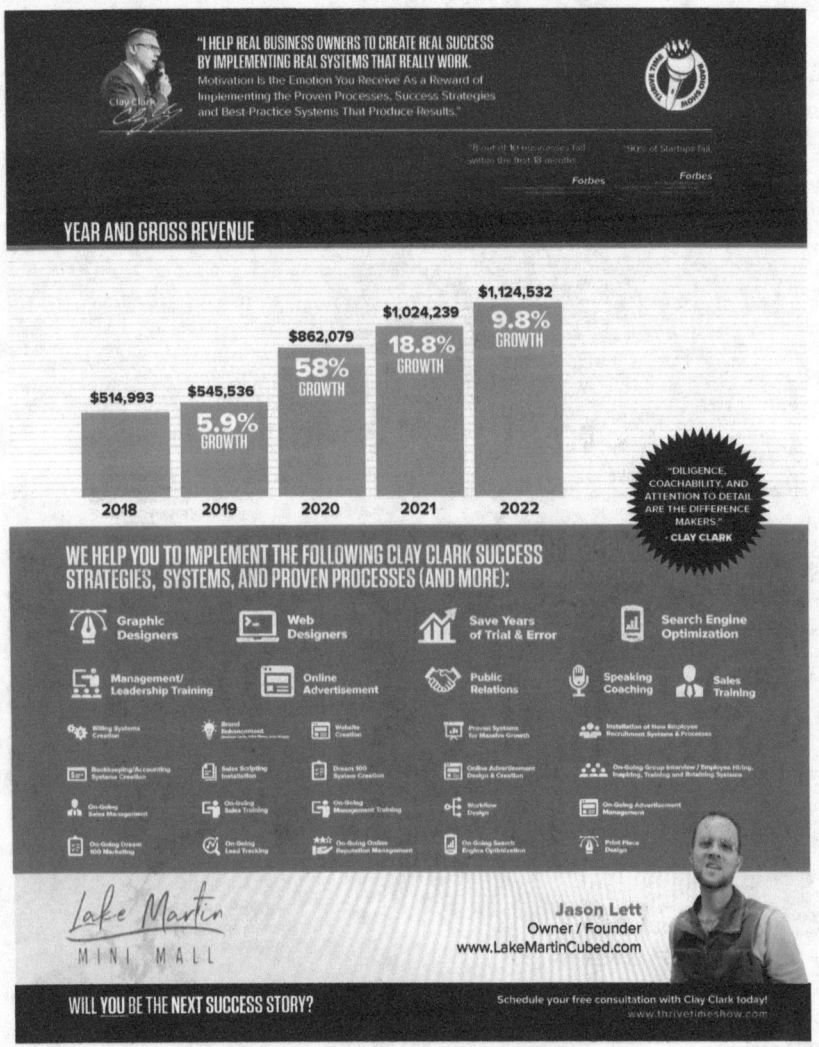

See thousands of real Clay Clark success stories, case studies, and client testimonials today at www.ThrivetimeShow.com

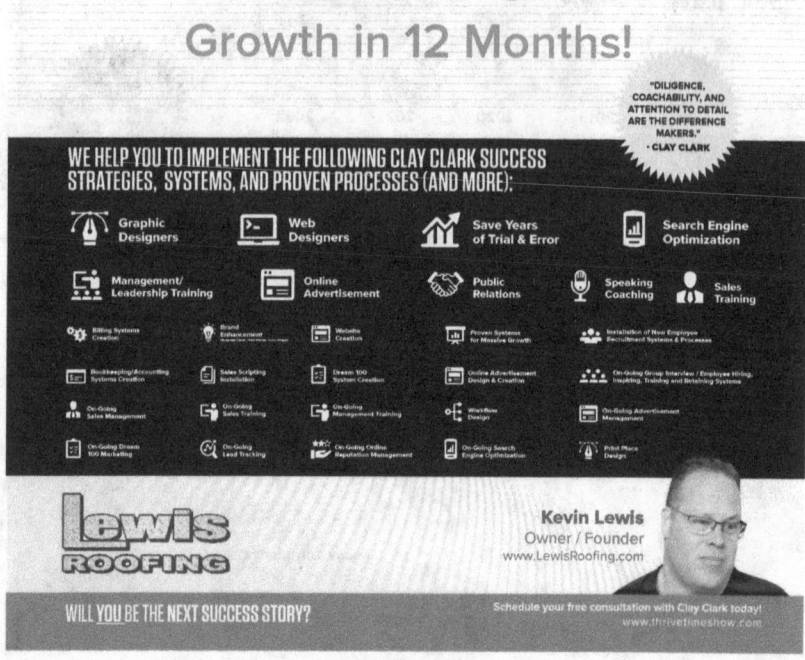

See thousands of real Clay Clark success stories, case studies, and client testimonials today at www.ThrivetimeShow.com

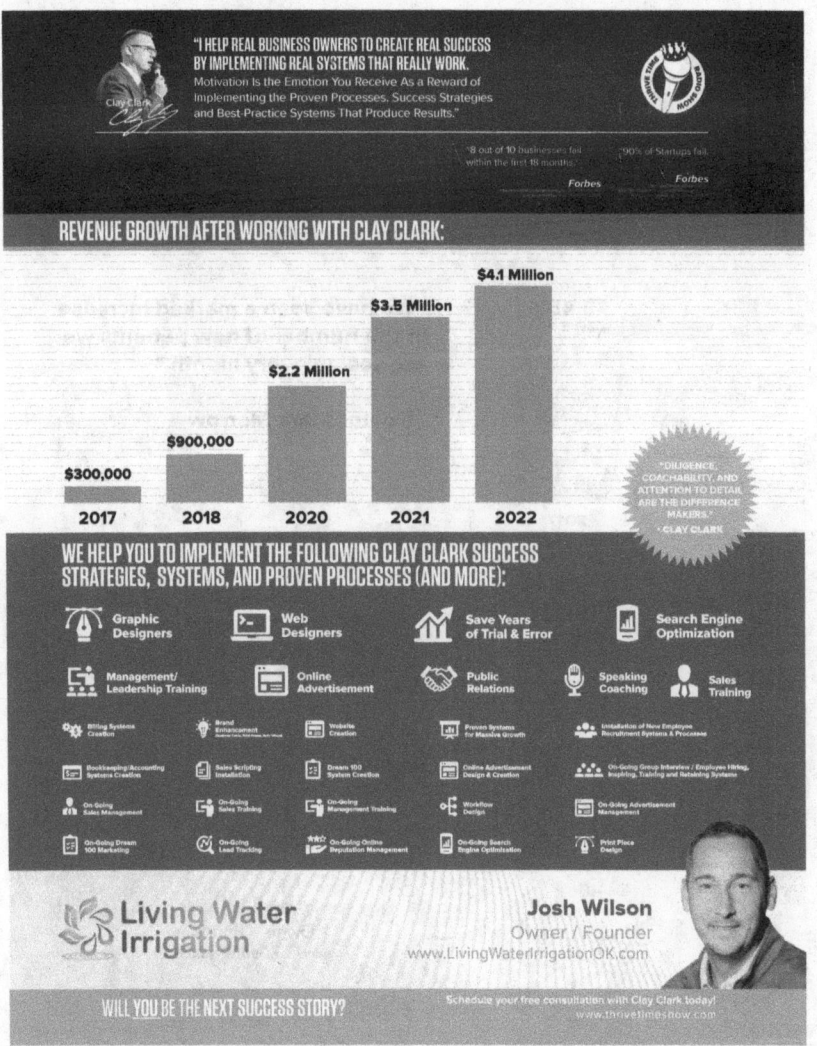

See thousands of real Clay Clark success
stories, case studies, and client testimonials
today at www.ThrivetimeShow.com

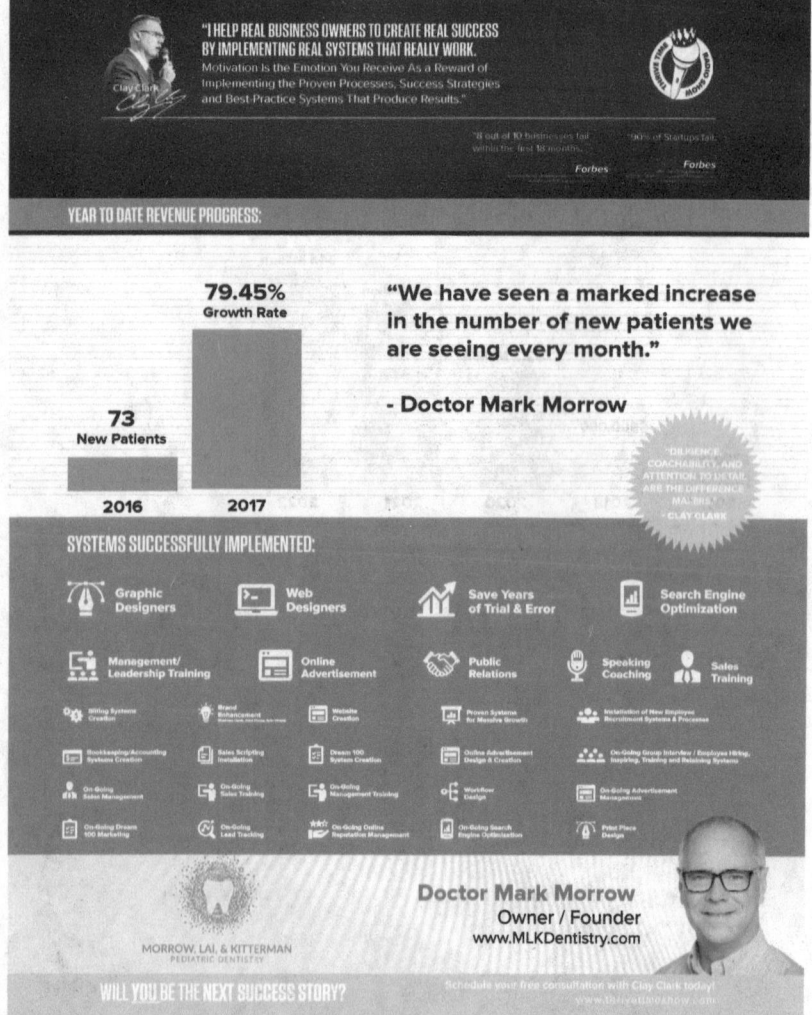

See thousands of real Clay Clark success stories, case studies, and client testimonials today at www.ThrivetimeShow.com

See thousands of real Clay Clark success stories, case studies, and client testimonials today at www.ThrivetimeShow.com

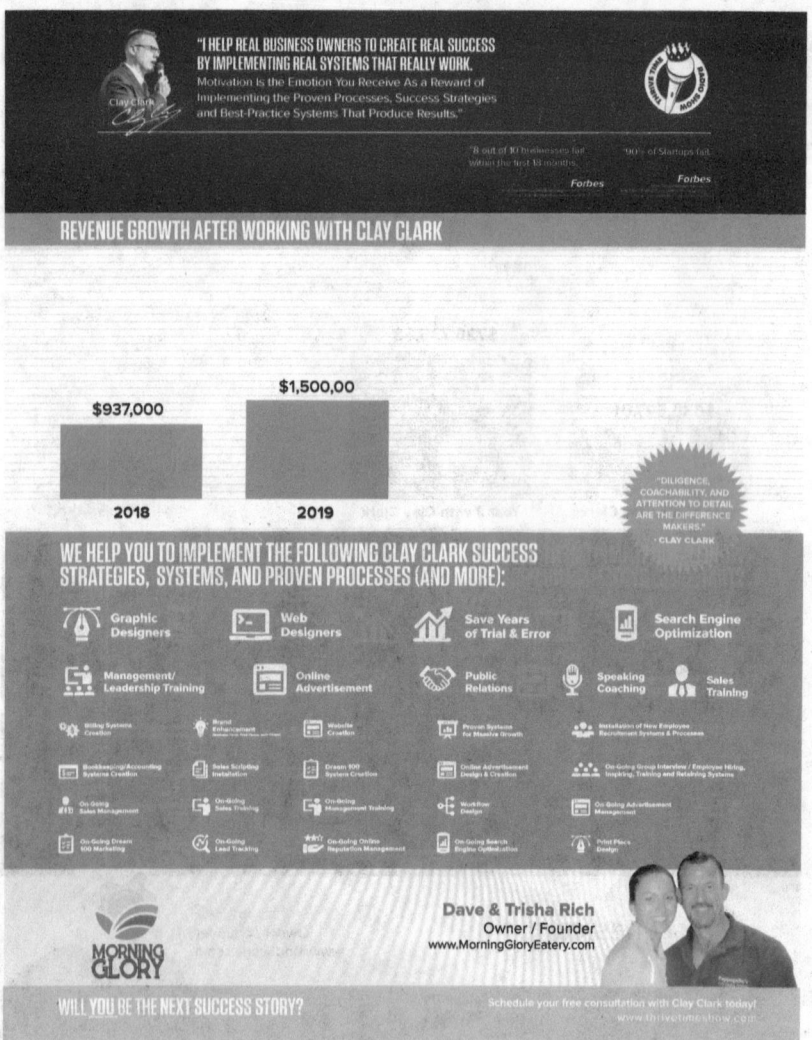

See thousands of real Clay Clark success stories, case studies, and client testimonials today at www.ThrivetimeShow.com

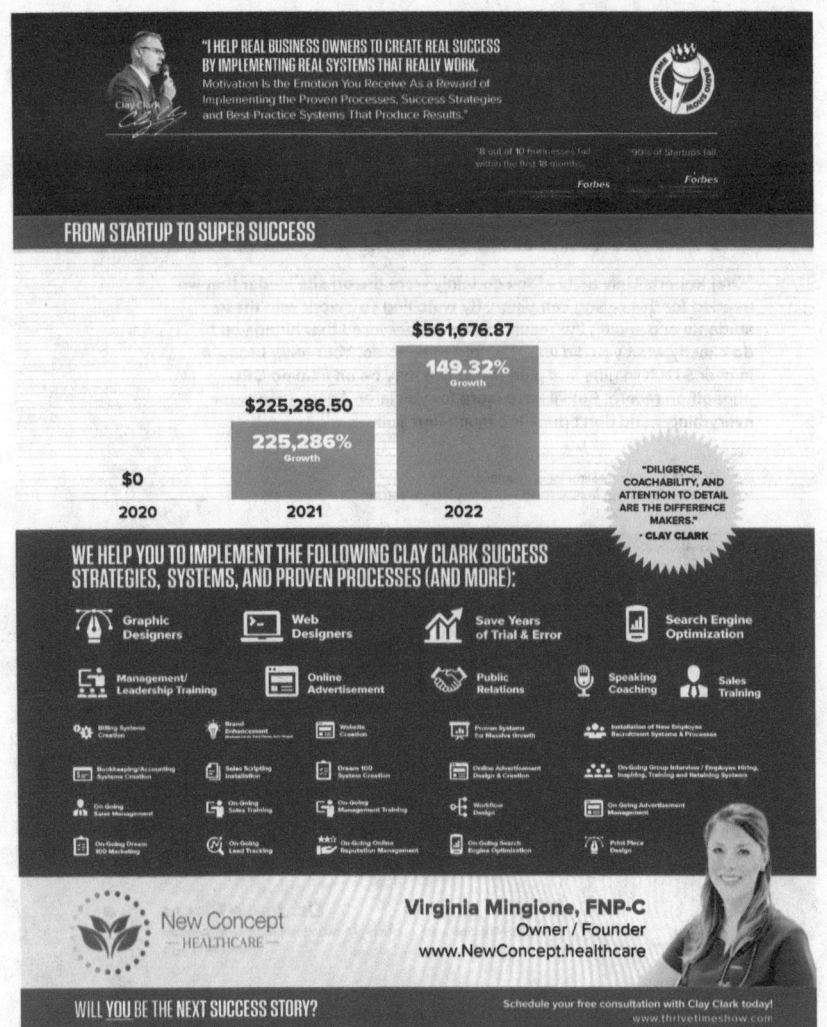

See thousands of real Clay Clark success stories, case studies, and client testimonials today at www.ThrivetimeShow.com

See thousands of real Clay Clark success
stories, case studies, and client testimonials
today at www.ThrivetimeShow.com

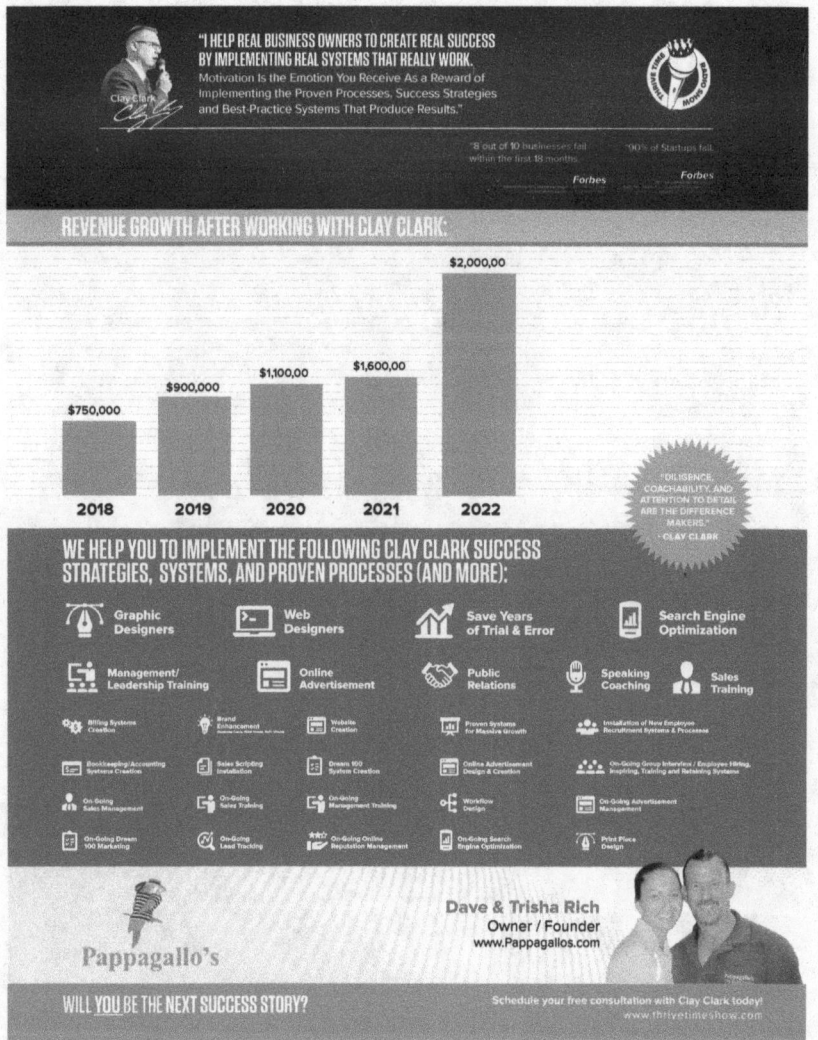

Want to open your own Make Your Dog Epic dog training business?
Learn how to have your own epic adventure by opening one of the
most affordable and turn-key dog training businesses on the planet!

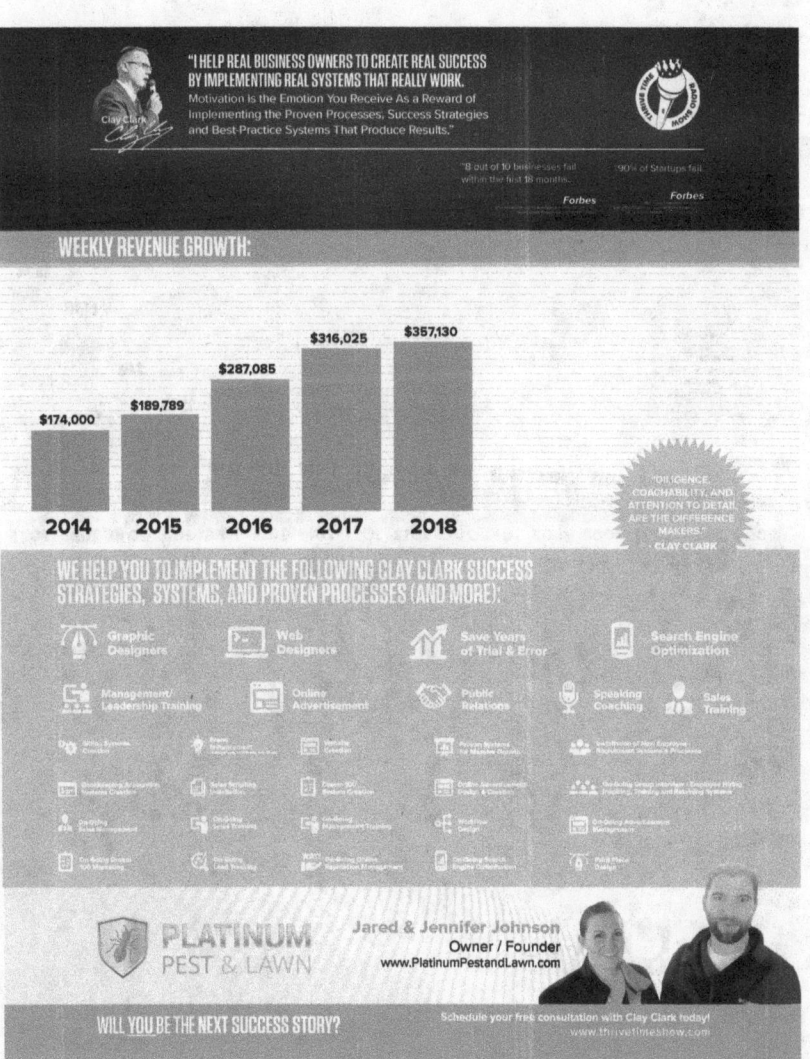

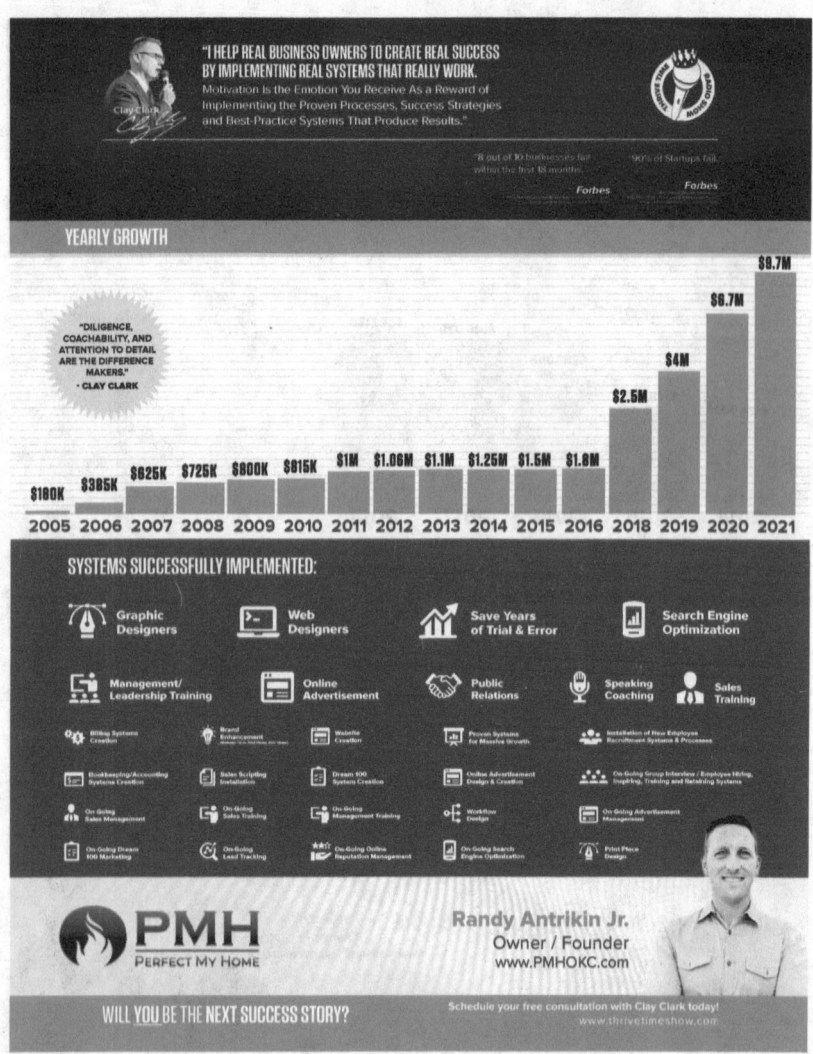

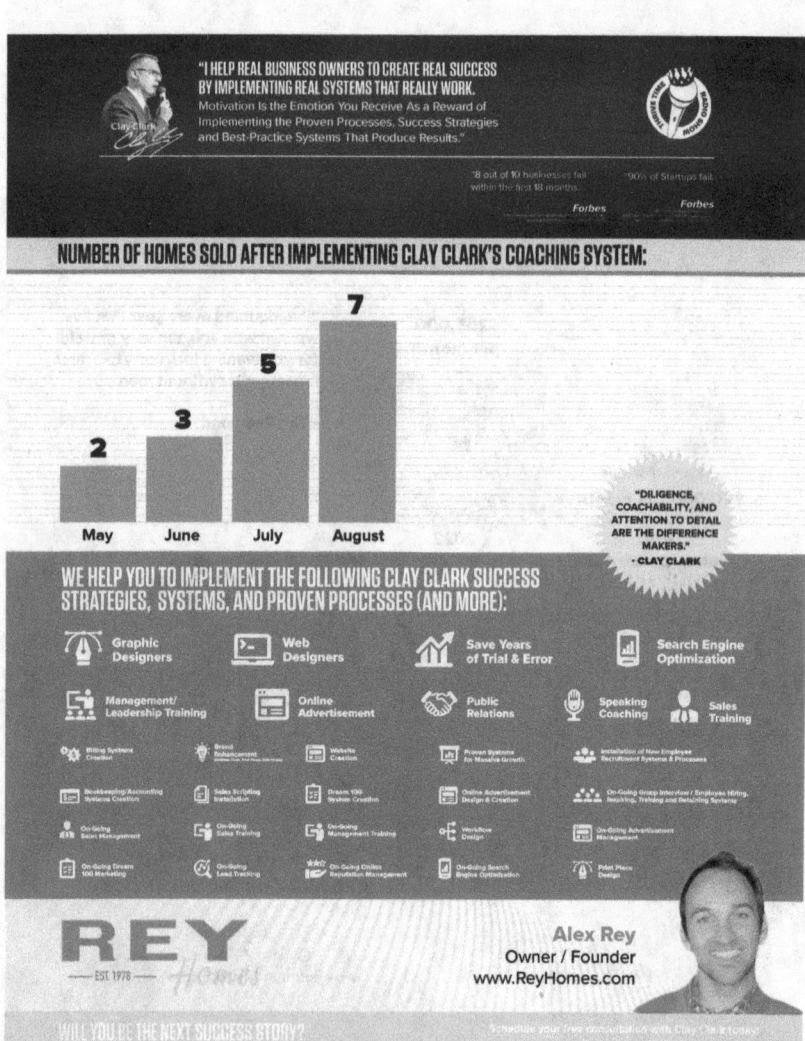

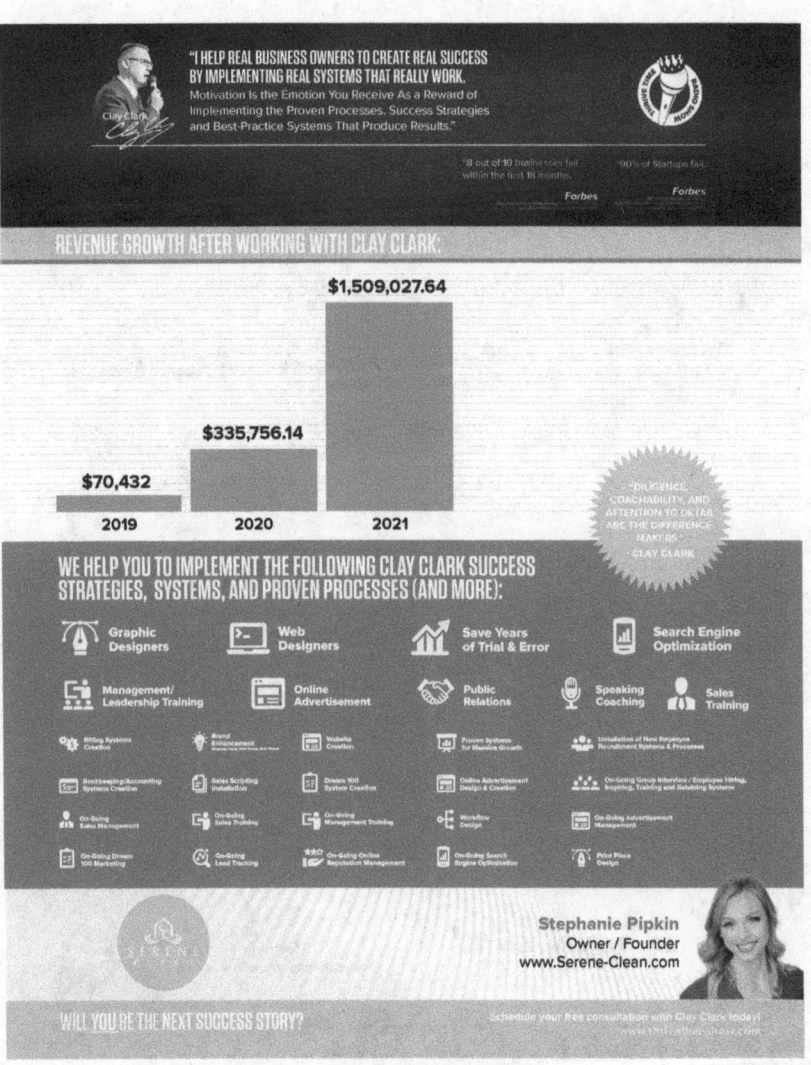

"I HELP REAL BUSINESS OWNERS TO CREATE REAL SUCCESS BY IMPLEMENTING REAL SYSTEMS THAT REALLY WORK. Motivation Is the Emotion You Receive As a Reward of Implementing the Proven Processes, Success Strategies and Best-Practice Systems That Produce Results."

Clay Clark

"8 out of 10 businesses fail within the first 18 months." *Forbes*

"90% of Startups fail." *Forbes*

IMPLEMENTING PROVEN SYSTEMS = SUCCESS

60% Growth Rate
IN 12 MONTHS

"DILIGENCE, COACHABILITY, AND ATTENTION TO DETAIL ARE THE DIFFERENCE MAKERS." - CLAY CLARK

WE HELP YOU TO IMPLEMENT THE FOLLOWING CLAY CLARK SUCCESS STRATEGIES, SYSTEMS, AND PROVEN PROCESSES (AND MORE):

 Graphic Designers
 Web Designers
 Save Years of Trial & Error
 Search Engine Optimization

 Management/ Leadership Training
 Online Advertisement
 Public Relations
 Speaking Coaching / Sales Training

Guy Shepherd
Owner / Founder
www.ShepherdAutomotive.com

WILL YOU BE THE NEXT SUCCESS STORY?

Schedule your free consultation with Clay Clark today!
www.thrivetimeshow.com

Want to open your own Make Your Dog Epic dog training business? Learn how to have your own epic adventure by opening one of the most affordable and turn-key dog training businesses on the planet!

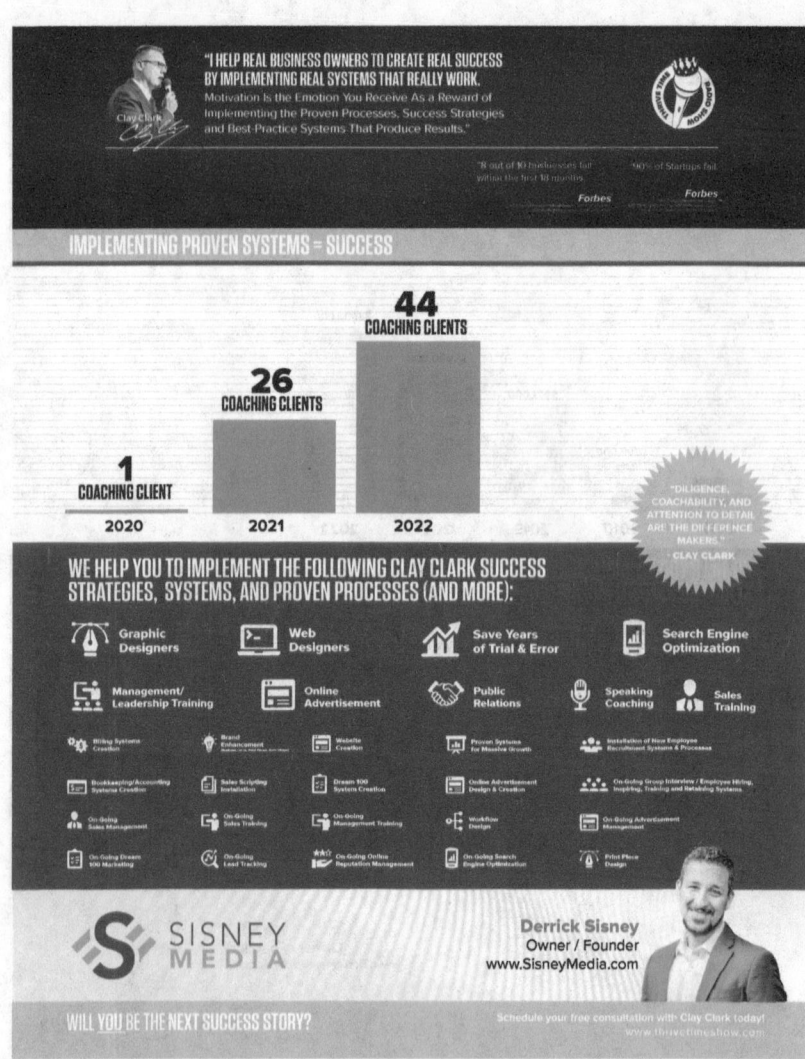

From start to $24 million of gross sales
(in just 18 months)

"From the very start everything that we do is a direct line from Clay and his team and all that they've done for us."

- Danielle Sprik

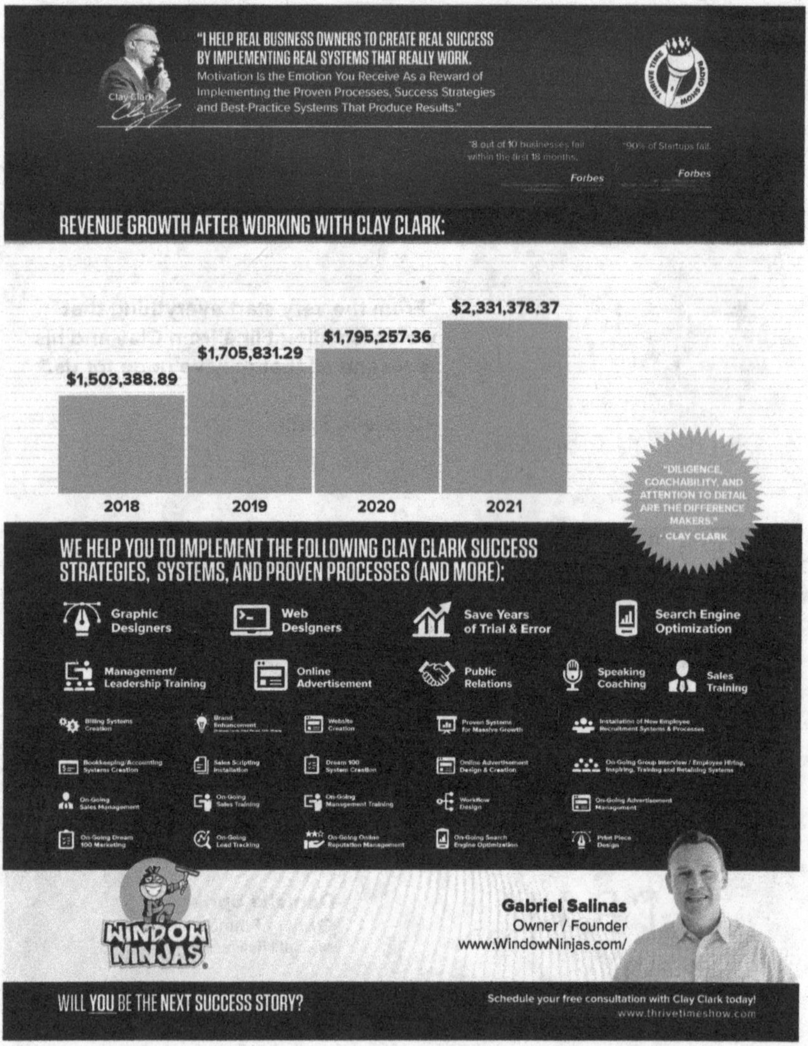

REVENUE GROWTH AFTER WORKING WITH CLAY CLARK:

$2,331,378.37 (2021)
$1,795,257.36 (2020)
$1,705,831.29 (2019)
$1,503,388.89 (2018)

2018   2019   2020   2021

"DILIGENCE, COACHABILITY, AND ATTENTION TO DETAIL ARE THE DIFFERENCE MAKERS."
- CLAY CLARK

WE HELP YOU TO IMPLEMENT THE FOLLOWING CLAY CLARK SUCCESS STRATEGIES, SYSTEMS, AND PROVEN PROCESSES (AND MORE):

- Graphic Designers
- Web Designers
- Save Years of Trial & Error
- Search Engine Optimization
- Management/ Leadership Training
- Online Advertisement
- Public Relations
- Speaking Coaching
- Sales Training

- Billing Systems Creation
- Brand Enhancement
- Website Creation
- Proven Systems for Massive Growth
- Installation of New Employee Recruitment Systems & Processes
- Bookkeeping/Accounting Systems Creation
- Sales Scripting Installation
- Dream 100 System Creation
- Online Advertisement Design & Creation
- On-Going Group Interview / Employee Hiring, Inspiring, Training and Retaining Systems
- On-Going Sales Management
- On-Going Sales Tracking
- On-Going Management Training
- Workflow Design
- On-Going Advertisement Management
- On-Going Dream 100 Marketing
- On-Going Lead Tracking
- On-Going Online Reputation Management
- On-Going Search Engine Optimization
- Print Piece Design

WINDOW NINJAS.

Gabriel Salinas
Owner / Founder
www.WindowNinjas.com/

WILL **YOU** BE THE **NEXT** SUCCESS STORY?

Schedule your free consultation with Clay Clark today!
www.thrivetimeshow.com

                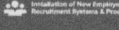 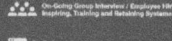   

Want to open your own Make Your Dog Epic dog training business?
Learn how to have your own epic adventure by opening one of the
most affordable and turn-key dog training businesses on the planet!

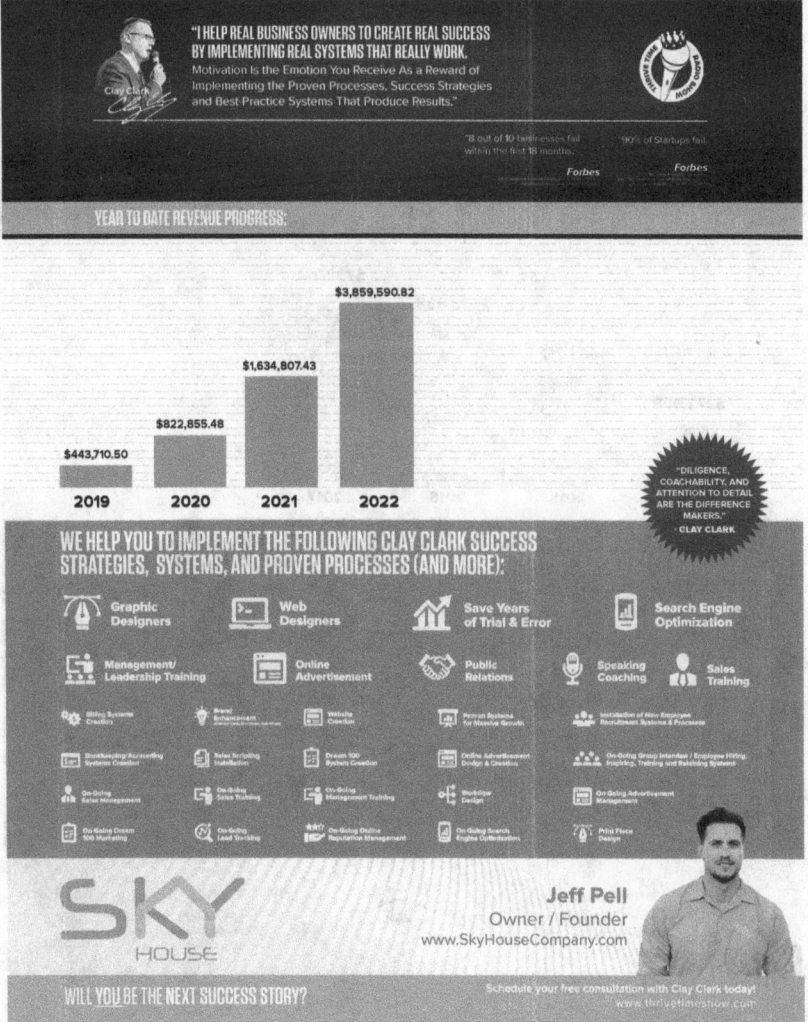

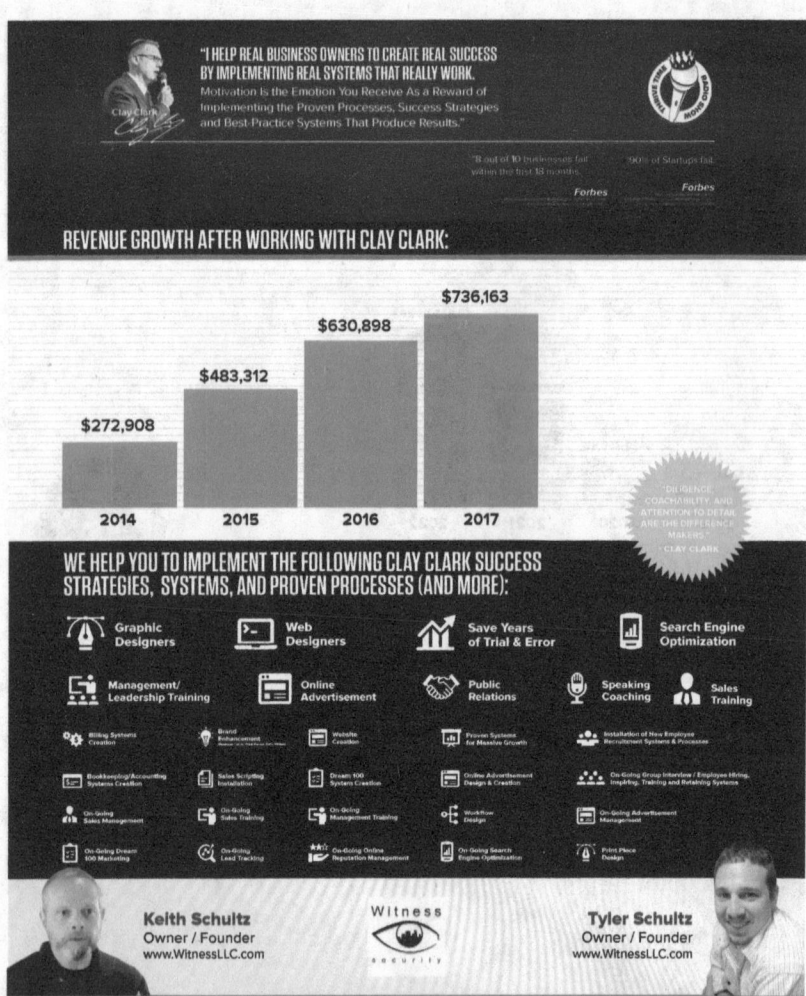

REVENUE GROWTH AFTER WORKING WITH CLAY CLARK:

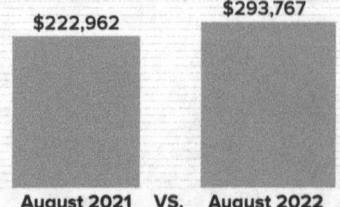

$222,962   **$293,767**

August 2021   VS.   August 2022

"DILIGENCE, COACHABILITY, AND ATTENTION TO DETAIL ARE THE DIFFERENCE MAKERS."
- CLAY CLARK

WE HELP YOU TO IMPLEMENT THE FOLLOWING CLAY CLARK SUCCESS STRATEGIES, SYSTEMS, AND PROVEN PROCESSES (AND MORE):

Graphic Designers · Web Designers · Save Years of Trial & Error · Search Engine Optimization

Management/ Leadership Training · Online Advertisement · Public Relations · Speaking Coaching · Sales Training

Tim Scott
Owners / Founders
www.LegacyLandscapeOK.com

WILL YOU BE THE NEXT SUCCESS STORY?

Schedule your free consultation with Clay Clark today!

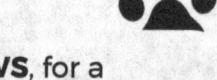

PAWS, for a
Notable Quotable

"Life is not a dress rehearsal. You must act now because we will all be dead soon and "someday" is not a day that appears on a standard calendar."

CLAY CLARK

(Former Oklahoma Young U.S. SBA Entrepreneur of the Year)

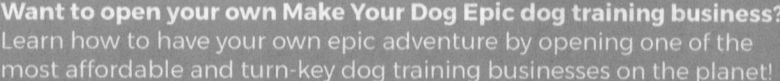

PAWS, for a
Notable Quotable

"No one lives long enough to learn everything they need to learn starting from scratch. To be successful, we absolutely, positively have to find people who have already paid the price to learn the things that we need to learn to achieve our goals."

BRIAN TRACY

(Best-Selling author, international speaker, sales trainer and business growth consultant)

Want to open your own Make Your Dog Epic dog training business?
Learn how to have your own epic adventure by opening one of the
most affordable and turn-key dog training businesses on the planet!